ADVANCE PRAISE FOR MATERNAL HOPE

"With this book, Seigle and Stevens offer a compassionate and much-needed contribution to the conversation about reproductive and maternal mental health. It's time we banish the silence, the stigma, and most of all, the shame that all too often accompany painful reproductive experiences. This book takes on these ubiquitous but still-taboo topics and offers the support women urgently need and deserve."

—JESSICA ZUCKER, PhD, psychologist and author of the award-winning *I Had a Miscarriage* and *Normalize It*

"As a physician, I have seen firsthand how isolating and complex the path to parenthood can be—especially when it doesn't follow a traditional route. *Maternal Hope* is a moving, necessary collection that amplifies the voices too often left out of the conversation. These stories are a reminder that every family has its own journey, and every journey deserves to be seen. As a mother of two, I've walked through my own seasons of uncertainty, joy, grief, and transformation. This book is a powerful offering of light, empathy, and resilience to anyone navigating the many layers of building and growing a family. May it be a balm for those still in the waiting, and a bridge for those ready to be seen."

—JESSICA SHEPHERD, MD, chief medical officer of Hers and author of *Generation M*

"*Maternal Hope* is a powerful reminder of the importance of community in difficult times. These moving stories reminded me that in the hardest moments of parenting, we are never truly alone. There is beauty in the mess, hope in the heartbreak, and power in sharing our journeys."

—AMANDA KLOOTS, celebrity fitness trainer and *New York Times* bestselling author of *Live Your Life*

"*Maternal Hope* is a testament to the quiet courage of people navigating some of life's most vulnerable moments. As a physician, I know how isolating these experiences can be. This book brings them into the light—with empathy, truth, and strength."

—NEEL SHAH, MD, chief medical officer, Maven Clinic

"The stories in *Maternal Hope* are medicine for the heart— tender, raw, and alive with the kind of truth that only emerges when we feel safe enough to be fully seen. This book honors the spiritual path of parents in all its forms: the longing, the loss, the miracles, and the quiet healings that shape us along the way. It's not just a collection of stories—it's a remembrance and a light in the dark. As a mother of two, this book was exactly what I needed to feel seen and less alone in my motherhood journey. Motherhood has shaped me into a brand new human (in every single way), and the depth of that truth is exactly the kind of magic that this book encompasses."

—JORDAN YOUNGER, founder and CEO of The Balanced Blonde and host of *The Balanced Blonde* podcast

"A collection as diverse as motherhood itself, filled with unique perspectives and experiences designed to make us all think and feel."

—**ZIBBY OWENS, podcast host, *Totally Booked with Zibby*, author, and bookstore owner**

"The heartfelt reflections in *Maternal Hope* are poignant, real, and all too relatable, and the honesty that pours forth in these pages is both compelling and comforting. I'm thrilled that Seigle and Stevens have added their voices and those of a dozen other thoughtful writers to this much-needed conversation. Brava!"

—**EVE RODSKY, *New York Times* bestselling author of *Fair Play* and *Find Your Unicorn Space***

"I wish I'd had this book in my early days of motherhood—or later, when I suffered a pregnancy loss and felt completely alone in my grief. Motherhood makes us desperate to connect with other moms in a raw, honest way, but when we are in crisis, it can feel too difficult to seek out these kinds of vulnerable (yet life-affirming) conversations. *Maternal Hope* is such a valuable resource. It's moving and healing while providing a safe space to explore the complex emotions of modern mothering. I am so grateful to the people in this book who shared their stories with us. More of this kind of connection, please! We need it now more than ever."

—**MARY CATHERINE STARR, author of *Mama Needs a Minute!* and artist behind @momlife_comics on Instagram**

"Becoming a parent can bring up big feelings, particularly if the path is difficult, painful, or complex. Seigle and Stevens offer hope by sharing honest, heartfelt reflections from real families who have been through dark moments and found light on the other side. *Maternal Hope* is a gift that will help readers feel less alone."

—MOLLIE WEST DUFFY, *Wall Street Journal*
bestselling coauthor of *No Hard Feelings*
and *Big Feelings*

"*Maternal Hope* gives voice to the often-unseen journey of building a family. As someone who knows the importance of storytelling to help people feel seen and supported as they navigate complex modern family-building journeys, I appreciate the compassionate and powerful approach this book takes to sharing these stories."

—ANDREA SYRTASH, relationships author
and editor-in-chief, pregnantish

"Family building is an odyssey of unique circumstance and emotion. For those whose journey has been marked by adversity, disappointment, or trauma, this book provides hope to all in its most raw and candid form. As a past fertility patient, it transported me back to my own journey and offered insights into what helps us all through family building: resilience."

—BEC HOLMES, PhD, senior vice president
of lab operations, CCRM Fertility

"*Maternal Hope* is a courageous and necessary book. As a mother, daughter, and leader, I know how hard—and how powerful—it is to name what others leave unsaid. This beautifully honest book offers validation, insight, and hope for all of us in the invisible challenges we navigate. It reminds us that our vulnerability and shared humanity fuel our resilience."

—SIMONE AHUJA, mother, innovation strategist, and bestselling author of *Disrupt It Yourself*

"From the heartbreak of loss to the quiet moments of hope, the stories within *Maternal Hope* perfectly capture the beautiful and messy complexity of trying to become a parent. Reading them, I felt both seen and moved. These stories are a testament to the resilience of the human spirit and the strength that can be found in even the darkest moments."

—CAITLIN WEAVER, bestselling author of *Such a Good Family*

MATERNAL
HOPE

MATERNAL HOPE

Stories of Unseen Struggles, Unexpected Resilience,
and the Untold Ways Families Are Made

CAMILLE ALI MANN
SEIGLE STEVENS

ALONE
NO MORE
PRESS

Maternal Hope: Stories of Unseen Struggles, Unexpected Resilience, and the Untold Ways Families Are Made

ISBN (hardcover): 979-8-9995419-0-1
ISBN (paperback): 979-8-9995419-1-8
ISBN (e-book): 979-8-9995419-2-5

Library of Congress Control Number: 2025915092

Cover design by George Stevens

Published by Alone No More Press, Chicago, Illinois

To the unseen, the unheard, the unspoken—
may these pages remind you that hope often blooms just out of view.

And to Isabel, Teddy, and Ava—
our reasons, our light.

In loving memory of Liv and Max.

CONTENTS

FOREWORD

WHITNEY BISCHOFF ANGEL

Whether you've found this book, or this book has found you, it doesn't matter. What matters is that *Maternal Hope* is now a part of your story. Like a comforting presence, it's here to guide you, support you, and remind you that you are not alone. This book speaks to the universal emotions of loss, love, fear, and joy, offering a space where they can coexist and be understood. No matter the path you've walked to get here, this book is here for you.

Within these pages, you'll find stories of resilience, hardship, and an unspoken understanding that stretches across every loss, every longing, and every dream delayed or shattered. These stories are raw and impactful, reaching deeply into your heart and moving you to tears. They are the voices of those who have walked through pain and emerged with hope, just as you may be striving to do. And while you may not have seen it during your darkest moments, I promise you, *Maternal Hope* is here now.

For me, the concept of maternal hope began at nineteen after the tragic and unexpected loss of my mother. Without her steady hand to guide me and with no father to lean on, I found myself navigating life's most formative years alone. At the time, I didn't fully understand what I was searching for. But looking back, I realize what I desperately longed for was something to reassure me that I would be OK, that peace could be found amidst heartache, and that I could make it through the grief of growing up without her. I was searching for hope.

In the following years, I learned I could find what I sought, not just in my own strength, but in the relationships and communities I went on to build.

When I was first cast on *The Bachelor*, I thought I was embarking on a bizarre path to find true love, something that now feels almost laughable but was so real to me at the time. What I discovered was something far more profound: a group of women from all walks of life, each with a unique background and story, yet united by one shared thing—our hopes for the future.

Behind the scenes, away from the cameras and glamour of filming, we opened up to each other in raw, real ways. These weren't moments designed for "the most dramatic season ever." They were late-night conversations, without microphones or bright lights, when we could just be ourselves, sharing our deepest hopes, whether they were dreams of travel, careers, family, or motherhood. These moments, to me, captured the true essence of reality TV: real women, facing real challenges, having real conversations about the choices we face and the power of supporting one another through it all.

That experience taught me something profound: The importance of these conversations is not limited to a select few. They're for everyone. Even in the midst of a reality TV show, surrounded by cameras and dramatic moments, we were talking about the most authentic, difficult, and personal experiences that shape our lives. And in doing so, we bonded.

After the show, the conversation didn't stop. With the support of some close friends and our new platform, a few of us ignited a movement. We took the bold step of openly sharing our decision to freeze our eggs—an often-taboo topic —beyond the confines of the *Bachelor* mansion and into the world. By doing so, we hoped to bring attention to an option that many women might not even know is available or may feel too intimidated to consider or talk about. We wanted to show that having these conversations is not just OK but crucial—and that making intentional choices for our futures, even in the face of uncertainty, is both necessary and empowering.

Maternal hope is not one-size-fits-all. It looks different for each person. For some, it might be hope for motherhood, fertility, or guidance through pregnancy and postpartum. For others, it may be hope to heal from past loss or find strength in the face of seemingly insurmountable challenges. It's for those navigating loss, yearning for community, or seeking guidance and healing in any form. It's for men and women, parents and non-parents alike because hope, in its purest form, is universal.

One powerful lesson my mother taught me, which has stayed with me through the years, is: "Choices are the hinges of destiny." This simple yet profound truth has guided me, especially in moments when I've questioned my purpose. She introduced this quote to me in the following email six weeks before her unexpected passing, reinforcing how our choices shape our path forward:

> *I get two inspirational messages each day on my computer. Here's my correlation of today's to you: "Choices are the hinges of destiny." You have choices to make every day—we all do—and this will continue for the rest of your life. Will you let obstacles define you, or will you continue to pursue your dream? Whitney, I have enough faith in you to move mountains, but you have to believe too. Please believe with me!*

Since then, that same unwavering faith guided me through every hardship and decision, shaped by both personal loss and professional purpose. I pursued my dream of becoming a nurse, dedicating nearly twenty years to reproductive endocrinology and infertility. Over the years since then, I've watched countless families navigate loss, healing, and hope, and in doing so, I've relayed the same hope that carried me through my own health and fertility struggles.

In May 2019, I was fortunate enough to welcome my son, Hayes, who arrived earthside on the anniversary of my mother's passing. It was a powerful reminder that hope, even when born from loss, knows no boundaries. Yet the years that followed forced me to confront the grief I had buried so long ago.

After a year of persistent chest pain, dismissed by multiple providers, I was faced with a life-threatening condition: cardiac tamponade, caused by a virus silently attacking my heart over the prior year. I was lucky to survive, but the recovery was far from easy.

During this time, the medications required to treat my heart kept me from the one thing I longed for most: clearance to try for another baby. As time ticked on, so did the pressure of my biological clock. A year later when my health finally stabilized, I was given the go-ahead to conceive. But that hope was soon shattered by a series of early miscarriages and an ectopic pregnancy, leading me to the question I'd asked so many times before: *Why me?* How could it be that a seasoned fertility nurse, with access to experts across the country, couldn't find a solution?

In an act to regain control, I thawed the eggs that I had frozen in 2013 as the backup plan I thought I would never need. The eggs thawed and fertilized, and I had some embryos to work with. For a brief moment, I felt in control again—until I faced a failed transfer. Once more, I found myself searching for something intangible, only to realize that what I had been searching for all along was the same thing I had longed for when I was nineteen: *hope*. Hope that I would be OK. Hope that I wasn't alone. Hope that there would be light in the darkness if I could just find the strength to look up.

And ultimately, that light shone brighter than I could've imagined. A few months later, we received the surprise of a lifetime: two pink lines. My husband, Ricky, and I welcomed our daughter, Brady, in August 2023.

My experiences as both a provider and patient sparked a deeper drive to help others beyond the clinic, recognizing the critical need for emotional, mental, and relational support during fertility, pregnancy, and the postpartum period. Inspired by the hope I had found, I took the leap to step away from the clinical setting and cofound my own company, Lily Concierge Consulting, to guide others through the often-complex path to parenthood in a healthcare system that feels increasingly mechanized. While it took me time to make this decision, I'm reminded that our lives are filled with complexities and uncertainties, yet somehow we're always guided to our purpose. And this choice has led me to mine.

The stories ahead are like mine—stories of profound, heart-wrenching challenges: the grief of miscarriage, the emptiness of stillbirth, the fragile hope of pregnancy after loss, and the courage it takes to pursue fertility treatments. These stories aren't confined to simple dimensions. They stretch beyond what we can fully see or understand. They transcend barriers of race, gender, socioeconomic status, and background. They reflect the complex emotions and struggles surrounding single parenting, same-sex couples, surrogacy, and choosing not to parent at all. And most importantly, they reflect that no matter how our journey unfolds, we are all in this together.

The hope I longed for as a young woman, scared of what lay ahead, is now the hope I share with you as you turn the pages. It is through pain that we often find our purpose, not only for ourselves but for others as well. It is in the sharing of our stories—the comfort we offer one another—that we begin to heal, find meaning, and move toward hope. As you read these stories and reflect on your own, may you find comfort, connection, and the kind of hope that knows no bounds. *Maternal Hope* is here to remind you that, in the end, we are all capable of navigating the uncharted waters of our lives, and that no matter how lost we feel at times, we are never truly alone.

Whitney Bischoff Angel, BSN, RN
Founding partner of Lily Concierge Consulting

INTRODUCTION

This is Liv. *Twenty-six-week preemie, day thirty-seven of life, NEC, E. coli, septic shock.*

That was how the medical team introduced Ali's daughter during their daily rounds in the NICU. Seven people in scrubs stood at Liv's bedside: the nurse, resident, fellow, attending, surgeon, anesthesiologist, and neo-nutritionist. Outside the hospital, the world was in chaos. A global pandemic had shuttered businesses, and protests filled the streets. Inside the hospital, the world of Ali and her husband, Tim, was collapsing too. For thirty-seven days, they had fought for Liv's survival while mourning the death of her twin brother, Max, who had passed away just one day after he was born.

The journey that brought Ali to this moment had been long and isolating. Infertility, IVF, high-risk twins, and a harrowing delivery were just the beginning. There is much more to Ali's story. The terrifying moments, like giving birth in an unexpected location and handing her infant to Tim as though they were in some surreal version of *The Lion King*. The moments of heartbreak, like planning cremation arrangements instead of birth announcements. And the moments of unexpected grace, like the packages of food, texts, and even toilet paper left on their doorstep by friends and neighbors who wanted to help.

Camille's journey could not have been more different, and yet she, too, knows what it's like to feel utterly alone. Her pregnancy came easily, and her delivery just before the pandemic hit was uneventful. On paper, everything should have been perfect. But when Camille brought her daughter home, the overwhelming weight of motherhood set in. Used to excelling at everything she did, she felt paralyzed by the demands of caring for her newborn. She had heard of postpartum depression but assumed it was something other people dealt with. But Camille's reality looked different than that of her friends, with their highlights posted on Instagram. She breastfed but felt more like a dairy cow than a mother. Friends asked about the baby's milestones but never about her own healing—both physical and emotional. When the pandemic quarantine began, the isolation became suffocating, and Camille found herself trapped in a relentless cycle of feedings, diaper changes, and naps. One day, she walked onto her roof deck and wondered if she had the strength to continue.

But she did. Slowly, step by step, Camille began asking herself a simple but powerful question: *What do I need in order to feel better?* That question became her lifeline.

Our stories are different, but the pain we've each felt—the loneliness, loss, and questioning of ourselves—is universal. When you're in the depths of despair, you're not looking for easy answers or tidy resolutions. You're looking for hope. You're looking for connection. And above all, you're looking for proof that you're not alone.

We know this because we've lived it. We searched for community in Facebook groups and hashtags. We found glimmers of understanding in TED Talks and Instagram captions. But what we couldn't find was a book—a collection of real, unvarnished stories about the messy, painful, and beautiful realities of parenthood. A book to remind us that, even in our darkest moments, others had walked this path before us and made it through. That's the book we needed.

And that's the book we've written.

Maternal Hope is a collection of deeply personal narratives by those who have navigated the types of challenges that often get buried in the shadows. The stories you will read in the pages ahead explore the many paths to parenthood—some chosen, some forced by life's unpredictability. They cover infertility, miscarriage, infant loss, postpartum depression, adoption, surrogacy, and the decision to remain child-free. They are stories of heartbreak and resilience, of despair and hope. They are not filtered or polished for social media; they are raw, honest, and real.

Unlike anthologies that feature celebrities or influencers with access to every resource imaginable, the voices in *Maternal Hope* belong to everyday people. People like us, and people like you. Their experiences are as varied as their backgrounds, but their stories share a common thread: the power of vulnerability and the strength found in connection.

We wrote this book to break the silence around the struggles of starting a family. To offer a hand to those who feel like they're drowning. To create a community within these pages for anyone who has ever felt isolated, unseen, or unsure of what comes next.

If you're holding this book, it's likely because you or someone you love is walking a hard road right now. We want you to know: You are not alone. There is hope. There is strength in sharing our stories, and there is healing in hearing yours echoed back to you. We hope that you'll join us on this journey. Together, we will find a way forward.

1

YOU ARE NOT ALONE: MY STORY OF MISCARRIAGE AND MOTHERHOOD

MONICA ROYER

Parenthood is a journey that brings some of life's greatest joys and also some of its most painful heartbreaks. As women, we're often encouraged to share the sweet, sunlit moments: the first ultrasound, the baby kicks, the nursery reveal. But I believe it's just as important to share the dark, lonely corners of this experience—to remind each other that we are not alone.

My own journey into motherhood began joyfully. My pregnancy with my daughter was healthy, and I delivered her without complication. That experience became the foundation of so much in my life—including the decision to launch Monica + Andy, a company inspired by her birth and built for the next generation of babies and parents like me, with a goal to be a parent's first friend.

I like to say this company was "born in a delivery room, not a boardroom," as I wanted my daughter—and all babies and their parents—to have access to the best quality and most helpful products. From day one, I also believed in the beauty of the sibling bond, which is why I included my brother's name. Andy and I are incredibly close, and it was that inspiration that became our brand's North Star: the idea that siblings could be best friends.

And so when I became pregnant a second time, I was overjoyed. The pregnancy felt familiar—the same exhaustion, the same nausea, the same relentless need to nap through the afternoon. But this time, life looked very different. I was running a rapidly growing company. I had a four-and-a-half-year-old daughter. And I had very little time to slow down.

Because of the way I was feeling—and the fact that my coworkers could see the difference in me—I revealed my pregnancy early. I didn't have the luxury of hiding it, so I told those around me. Coffee suddenly made me gag. I looked pale and drained. Sharing the news felt necessary, but also joyful. I was excited.

Then came the day of the routine ultrasound. I remember lying on the table, the cold gel on my stomach, waiting for that comforting sound: a heartbeat. But instead, the screen stayed silent. I stared at the monitor while the technician moved the wand, keeping her voice soft as she carefully chose her next words. I could tell something was wrong, even before she said it. "The heartbeat isn't there," she said gently. "Maybe it's too early to detect it ... but we'll need to schedule a follow-up."

The days between that appointment and the next felt like a lifetime. I read everything I could get my hands on—stories of hope, stories of miracles. I wanted to believe I might be one of them. But at the follow-up, the silence returned. This time, there was no "maybe."

As they wheeled me into the operating room, I felt like I was walking through fog. I remember staring up at the lights on the ceiling and thinking: *This is my fault. Maybe I worked too hard. Why didn't I see the signs? I should have known better. I should have done better.*

Miscarriage, to me in that moment, felt like failure. Like I had made a mistake, and now I was paying the price.

I'd already told so many people about the pregnancy. For

some women in my situation, that could be seen as a liability, as they can't shrink away from bad news over their pregnancy loss. But for me, instead of regretting that decision, it became a lifeline. The outpouring of love and support from friends and family carried me through. And even more than that, it was their stories—of loss, of grief, and eventually, of healing —that lit the path forward for me.

One friend—who I had no idea had previously miscarried —sent me a message I'll never forget. She said: "You are not broken. This is not your fault. And you will survive this, even when it doesn't feel like you will." Her words became an anchor for me. Another friend had experienced multiple losses and still found the strength to try again. I thought of her often in the quiet, empty moments after my surgery.

Then I had another devastating experience: my second miscarriage. And a third. Both times, I knew what was coming. Once I got the news, I braced myself, going through the motions with the weary familiarity of someone who had been there before. I had walked this road. I knew the anesthesia. I recognized the smell of the operating room. But the pain was no less sharp. If anything, the second and third losses made it feel like a pattern—like something might be wrong with me. My first miscarriage had felt like a fluke. The next two were harder to explain away.

And of course, the questions continued: "When will you give her a sibling?" "Isn't it time for another?" Innocent, well-meaning comments that struck like tiny knives. They didn't know about the children I never got to meet. They didn't know how hard I was trying.

Through it all, I kept telling my story. Not in a big, performative way, but in real conversation. When people asked about babies or pregnancy, I didn't lie or deflect. I told them about my losses. About the pain. About the little lives that existed only in my heart.

The experience of losing three children to miscarriage—

and sharing about it with others—made me whole again, in a way I didn't expect. I've realized that I'm not defined by my ability to conceive or carry a child. I'm not "less than" because I experienced miscarriage. And neither are you.

To anyone reading this who has experienced a miscarriage, infertility, a child with severe health complications, or an unconventional path to motherhood, I want you to know this: You are not alone. You are not broken. And there is nothing you need to hide.

We deserve to be seen in all parts of our parenthood journey—not just the moments worthy of Instagram. We deserve to be supported, held, and celebrated, even in the midst of heartbreak.

Hearing the stories of others who have struggled has helped me heal. Telling my own story has too. I wish the same comfort and healing for you, and I hope that together we can change the narrative—one brave, honest conversation at a time.

Discussion Questions

The author emphasizes the importance of sharing the painful parts of motherhood, not just the joyful moments. She also found strength and healing through the stories of others who had experienced similar losses.

1. How does the pressure to present a "perfect" narrative of parenthood affect someone's ability to grieve, connect, and heal? In what ways can we create safer spaces for more honest conversations around miscarriage and loss?

2. How do shared stories and vulnerability help to break the stigma around miscarriage and infertility? Have you ever experienced healing or connection through someone else's openness, or by sharing your own story?

2

THE GIFT OF PERSPECTIVE IN A LIFE UNEXPECTED

DR. SONAL PATEL

I walked more than three miles the evening before Radha was born. Despite having a relatively easy pregnancy, I was tired of the excessive peeing, discomfort, and poor sleep and was impatient for my baby girl to arrive. Plus, I had four equally eager, soon-to-be grandparents sitting together on the sofa of our downtown Chicago apartment, watching Indian television loudly every evening for the week leading up to the delivery.

I pleaded with my ob-gyn for an induction, but it was not recommended. So I took matters into my own hands and began the slow but deliberate waddle around our apartment floor. My husband, Vibhav, joined me on the walk for some much-needed alone time and to escape the smell of curry from the grandparents' cooking, which was starting to penetrate the walls of the apartment. I went to bed that night feeling exhausted but accomplished. Then around 3:30 a.m., I woke to the first pangs of labor. I remember thinking in that moment that my life would never be the same, and I suddenly felt nostalgic for the simpler life I was giving up.

Vib and I made our way to the labor and delivery ward at the hospital, which was connected by a short bridge to the children's hospital where I was completing a fellowship in pediatric gastroenterology. It was an unusually warm, sunny day in late January 2016, which I took to be a good omen. After just over an hour of pushing, Radha was born to the sounds of Hindu hymns playing on a loop in the delivery room.

Her body was perfect in every way, from her soft black hair down to her toenails. She had ten fingers, ten toes, two eyes, one nose. Divine. I never knew it was possible to fall in love with something—someone—so instantly. Suddenly, my life was now committed to raising this beautiful creature.

Two days later as we drove her home, I felt like Radha had always been a part of our family, and that life prior to her birth was unimaginable, despite only having known her for forty-eight hours. The grandparents greeted the three of us upon our arrival, swooping Radha up with an outpouring of absolute adoration and love in its purest form.

The first year of Radha's life was bliss. We marveled at how quickly she was growing and developing. I recall her eyelashes becoming noticeably longer on what seemed to be a daily basis. I would assess her developmental milestones periodically to ensure she was on target, which she always was.

As the weather got warmer, we ventured out into downtown Chicago to enjoy the riverwalk, parks, and outdoor restaurants. Radha always seemed to draw people to her. Maybe it was her gorgeous hair, plump cheeks, or stunning eyes that made people flock nearer. She was the crown jewel of our family and could command attention with just one look.

By ten months of age, Radha was pulling up in order to stand and starting to walk while holding on to furniture, which is termed "cruising." I thought it would be a matter of weeks before she was toddling around.

Then fifteen months came and went with no improvement in walking. Our pediatrician, however, wasn't concerned. He wiggled Radha's legs during an appointment and stated, "This child does *not* have a neurological issue"—one of the many misstatements that is forever burned into my memory. He recommended seeing a physical therapist and an orthopedic surgeon, both of whom found nothing that merited concern.

By the summer of 2017, I had finished my fellowship and joined the hospital where I had trained as an attending physician, and Vibhav had finished his own medical training. We spent the summer weekends traveling to visit family and friends while also making a dedicated effort to spend our weekday evenings at the park where Radha could see other children in their most active states. We worked on building her core strength, balance, and agility by playing on various playground installations, almost as if we were circuit training.

By eighteen months of age, Radha was stronger than she had ever been. She was walking with just the slightest hold of a hand, but still not independently. I again reached out to our pediatrician, this time requesting a neurology referral. He complied but stressed that he did not believe anything concerning was going on.

We saw the neurologist in November 2017, who felt with much certainty that Radha had "vestibulosensory issues," which essentially meant she didn't like the feeling of being unstable or falling. He was so confident in his diagnosis that he wrote, "I see no medical reason why this child is not walking," in his progress note.

All the while, my anxiety continued to build. Something was going on with Radha, but neither I, nor the multitude of pediatric subspecialists who had evaluated her, could explain why she wasn't walking. I remember seeing a child running at the park and thinking to myself that Radha would never be able to do that, despite doctors telling me she was completely fine. Vib and I would have dreams at night of Radha walking, giving us a brief moment of serenity and relief, only to awake in the morning and realize that nothing had changed; we were still living amongst our fears.

In January 2018, we took Radha to Disney World for her second birthday. This was the last time that I remember being truly at ease, putting my fears about Radha's walking aside for a short while. We spent four incredible days at the parks, but when we returned home, Radha was no longer interested in drinking milk from her sippy cup. Whereas normally she would pound back her six-ounce cup in the morning and again before bed, suddenly it took her an hour to drink just four ounces. She had also begun storing food in her mouth instead of swallowing, something she'd never done previously. On one occasion after dinner, I opened her mouth and found the few bites she'd eaten smashed into her palate.

Our fears renewed, we met with a neuromuscular neurologist at the end of January 2018. Having had no hint of concern from any of Radha's previous providers, we went into the appointment relatively calm and level-headed. But at the end of the assessment, the neurologist reported that Radha's nerve conduction, or how fast signals traveled from her brain to her muscles, was delayed—by a lot.

My heart shot into my throat. I had to prop myself up against the wall because I was so overwhelmed. *What does this mean?* I wondered. *Will she ever walk? And why are we only finding out about this now after almost a year of concern?*

From there, our medical quagmire only deepened, accompanied by an insurance nightmare. While the neurologist recommended genetic testing, our insurance company required preauthorization for the test, which could take weeks. Our other option was to pay thousands of dollars out of pocket. On top of this, we had requested a brain MRI to cover all our bases, which the neurologist did not think was necessary at the time.

As we navigated all this, Radha began exhibiting new, more concerning symptoms. Her overall oral intake had decreased substantially, and she was losing weight rapidly. She began having episodes of reflux and vomiting, which had not happened since she was an infant. Her hand strength was weakening, and she dropped objects easily.

The neurologist again explained away all my concerns. She said that children can become picky eaters, leading to fluctuations in weight gain; milk intake decreases over time as kids get older; and so on.

I had never felt so dismissed in my entire life, and I was a pediatric subspecialist speaking with another pediatric subspecialist. We were not being heard or regarded by the people we were seeking out for help, and this compounded the stress that was already eating away at our well-being.

Still dealing with the insurance nightmare of preauthorization for genetic testing, I continued to push for the MRI—as both a doctor and a mother. The neurologist relented. As I handed Radha over to the MRI nurse, I could feel an ominous force hovering over us. After it was finished, Vib went to the radiology reading room to ask about her results. The radiologist reviewed the images with him.

"The findings are consistent with leukodystrophy," the doctor told Vib before clarifying, "a disease affects the white matter of the brain."

Vib returned to find me and Radha in the recovery room, appearing shocked and confused. I immediately researched the term *leukodystrophy* only to read the words "rapid, progressive deterioration," "early death," and even "euthanasia" on one website. That was all I needed to know.

I ran from the recovery room to the least public nook I could find. My tears were flowing so heavily that I could barely see in front of me as I ran.

Words cannot describe the darkness of that day, and how our lives were forever changed in such a short moment. The day was Friday, April 13, 2018, the anniversary of which still haunts me every year.

After the MRI, we spent an entire weekend in agony, with no idea what type of horrific disease Radha had or what we could do—if anything—to help her. On Monday, we learned Radha had the late-infantile type of metachromatic leukodystrophy, a disease characterized by rapid, progressive loss of motor skills, weakness, inability to eat by mouth, vision loss, and early death. We were told that children with late infantile MLD typically pass by age five.

These words from the doctor seemed surreal, impossible. There was no treatment for the condition. My daughter had at most three more years to live. I gasped to breathe as the doctor left the room, then Vib, Radha, and I pulled close together while he and I sobbed quietly.

After returning home, I called my sister, Neelam. "It's terminal," I told her. "There's nothing we can do to stop this from progressing." We both cried.

"You need to move to Atlanta with us," she finally said. "We will do this together. We will take care of Radha as a family." Those words offered so much hope on a day when our world was crumbling around us and we could hardly stand on our own two feet.

Vib and I are different when it comes to coping with adversity. After Radha's diagnosis, he found solace in talking with a countless number of his closest friends for hours on end about the previous year's journey. I, on the other hand, could not even bring myself to tell my own parents. It was just too painful. I called exactly one of my best friends—after weeks of avoidance—and somehow verbalized the anguish, which was consuming me. At that point, I could not invest the emotional energy needed to grieve. My daughter and my family needed me to be their strength, and I was unwilling to dive into the deepest layer of sadness from which I was uncertain I could resurface.

I went back to work the very next day after that tragic doctor's visit. I didn't know what else to do.

Vib, on the other hand, took a leave of absence from work for several weeks and reached out to every contact he had to research possible options for treatment. He discovered an ongoing enzyme replacement trial in Europe run by Shire Pharmaceuticals, and although it was closed to new patient enrollments, we sent a barrage of phone calls and emails pleading with them to enroll Radha in the trial. We petitioned Shire and gathered more than one hundred thousand signatures from people worldwide in a matter of weeks, all asking that Radha be given the experimental treatment in order to try to save her life. They still refused.

Shortly after Radha's diagnosis, my sister, Neelam, gave me some unsolicited advice: She told me I needed to have another baby. She said I needed something to look forward to in the future, something to keep me positive. At the time, I was angry she would suggest this when our emotions about the diagnosis were still so raw. But the more I thought about it, the more I realized she was right.

But the only way we could ensure our next child would be free of any of the MLD-causing genes was to do in vitro fertilization with pre-implantation genetic testing. We figured, why not? We'd already met our total out-of-pocket expenses for 2018. This would be a small way to say "screw you" to Blue Cross and Blue Shield of Illinois. So we started the process prior to leaving Chicago.

By this point, Radha's oral intake was minimal. It took her two hours to eat half a cup of lentils and rice. She was dehydrated and unable to consume enough calories by mouth to keep her alive. She needed a gastrostomy tube (G-tube), otherwise known as a feeding tube. Of all the procedures that Radha had, this was the hardest for me to deal with. I'm a pediatric gastroenterologist, and G-tube management is an integral part of my job. But seeing my own daughter as a medically fragile child, unable to feed herself, almost broke me.

We moved to Atlanta and in with my sister four days after Radha's G-tube surgery—with no jobs, dwindling savings due to astronomical medical expenses, and no permanent home. By June of that summer, Radha was no longer able to sit upright independently. By July, she had stopped speaking—all of this only three months after her diagnosis.

Shortly after we arrived in Atlanta, my sister had some friends over. I remember talking with a few couples about their recent vacations, kids' summer activities, and busy jobs and realizing I had absolutely nothing to contribute to the conversation. I left the gathering and took Radha to our bedroom to be on our own. It was a moment when I felt completely isolated and alone.

Toward the end of August 2018, I flew back to Chicago to begin my IVF stimulation cycle. While I was there, I intentionally avoided the West Loop of downtown Chicago where we used to live. I didn't visit any of our favorite restaurants or meet up with any friends. I wanted to go unrecognized in the city where I had lived for the past five years. I was still not ready to grieve.

After the egg retrieval and fertilization, the embryos were sent out for genetic testing. Only one came back negative for genetic mutations that cause MLD. His name is now Shyam, and he is a feisty, energetic nineteen-month-old.

Before Shyam was born, Radha was granted a Wish Trip from the Make-A-Wish Foundation. We went back to Disney World for the second time in less than a year, but this time under vastly different circumstances. During our first trip, I had held Radha's hand as she walked toward a fountain at EPCOT Center. This time, I pushed her wheelchair to the same fountain. It was hard to acknowledge how much things had changed in less than a year. Still, seeing the joy in Radha's eyes as she watched the parades and her excitement when she met the Disney character Moana was priceless.

Since this trip, I have tried my best to live in the moment.

Second by second, minute by minute, hour by hour. Living to extract as much joy out of a single day as possible, even on the hard ones.

Balancing a newborn and Radha's care, we held on until the summer of 2019, when Vib learned of a new enzyme replacement trial that was starting in the United States. The closest trial centers were in Pittsburgh, Pennsylvania, and by October, Radha had been officially enrolled in the study. Enrollment meant Radha would undergo an infusion of the enzyme every week for two years.

For the first three months of 2020, we flew to Pittsburgh weekly. Shyam was only four months old at the time, so in addition to all of Radha's medical equipment and supplies, I was also packing a breast pump and bags to store breast milk. It was a busy, crazy time, but we were thrilled at the prospect of halting further progression of Radha's disease with this experimental drug. And while tiring, those weekly flights helped me realize how truly beautiful humanity can be.

Over the weeks, people started recognizing Radha in the airport in her distinctive blue stroller insert. We shared pieces of her story with the people we met along the way, explaining why we were traveling so frequently. The gate check luggage worker and airport shop employee prayed for Radha and gave her their best wishes and blessings. The gate agent in Pittsburgh would watch for us every week and ensure that we had extra help to board the plane. Even passengers on the plane would offer help if I ever seemed to be struggling. I never expected to receive so much support and outright love from random strangers, but these experiences helped me to realize that humans at their core are inherently good.

Then, the COVID-19 pandemic hit. I received a call from the research study coordinator who said the hospital was no longer accepting patients who flew to Pittsburgh via commercial airlines. Enter Angel Flight Soars, an organization consisting of volunteer pilots who fly patients to medical appointments free of charge on their own personal airplanes. These amazing people, real-life guardian angels, arranged a weekly private flight to Pittsburgh for Radha and me until a local trial site fortuitously opened in Atlanta. Had it not been for Angel Flights, Radha would have missed almost a month worth of infusions.

The 2020 year flew by for us despite the pandemic. Radha stayed out of the hospital for an entire year and even began regaining some of the motor skills she'd lost. One particular day stands out to me, when Radha suddenly began bending her knees and rocking side to side while on her back, something she hadn't done in more than two years. As she did it, she smiled as though she'd been tricking us the whole time.

This unexpected journey has been a mixed bag of emotions and events. Things have happened that seemed coincidental but maybe were actually destined. My previous beliefs in religion, existence, life purpose, and afterlife have all been upended. Radha's illness has devastated us to the core and is something from which we'll never completely recover. However, I see the strength in my darling little girl. I feel her eagerness to greet me every morning, and I know the extent of her tremendous power. It is from her that I receive the courage to carry on with her fight.

I still experience feelings of isolation, resentment, and even jealousy toward people who have more traditional parenting experiences. That said, I acknowledge that every person, no matter how perfect their life may seem, has been through hardship. I have good days and bad days. My sadness often erupts in the form of anger and lands on the people I love the most. I hate myself for this but am working toward being more open and honest about my pain.

In my clinical practice, I frequently care for patients who are medically fragile, some with G-tubes or global developmental delays. The families of these children are true unsung heroes. It's hard enough to be a parent of a typically developing child, and the work that goes into caring for a medically fragile child often exceeds that which a single person can do on their own.

I've had the opportunity to walk on both sides of the caregiving street. I've sat in the same exam room as a provider one day and as a parent with my child the next. This dichotomy is oftentimes difficult to process; however, I know for certain that caring for Radha has made me a better physician.

Looking for the silver lining in this unexpected life, I realize I've been given the gift of perspective. I cherish moments as much as possible, knowing that they're fleeting. I have the utmost gratitude for my resources, support, and educational background, which I rely on to care for my daughter with the understanding that many people are in desperate need of a fraction of what I have. Finally, I recognize that every person on this earth has their own battle to fight, their own struggle and strife. This, after all, is the human experience—and something that unites us all.

Our ride with Radha has been wild and is not over yet. When we first learned of her diagnosis, my aunt sternly said to me, "Don't ever feel sorry for yourself." This has stuck with me and helped to normalize our new way of life as we move forward. Radha has made me a better person and given me so much insight into what really matters in life. I am ever grateful for the opportunity to be her mother.

Discussion Questions

The author's vision for her perfect life is upended when her daughter, Radha, is diagnosed with a terminal illness. She and her husband marshal all their resources to seek and lobby for experimental treatment in order to keep Radha alive. They are ultimately successful but experience a roller coaster of emotions and experiences along the way.

1. Sonal goes from thinking her daughter's illness is terminal to finding a way to keep her alive with limitations that require lots of care. How do you think her feelings about her circumstances may have changed during the course of this emotional roller coaster?
2. Soon after Radha's diagnosis, the author's sister tells her she needs to have another baby to gain something positive to focus on. Would you have given the same advice? Why or why not?
3. The author talks about how caring for Radha taught her to live in the moment and try to extract as much joy as possible out of a single day, even the hard ones. Have you ever managed to find joy even in the midst of hardship? How did you do this?

3

LIV LIFE TO THE MAX

ALI MANN STEVENS

Liv is my firstborn daughter. Max is my firstborn son. They've never lived at home with my husband and me. Instead, they live permanently in our hearts and souls.

I've always known life is filled with surprises, both good and bad. Prior to becoming a parent, I'd been forced to do some deep soul searching and understood sooner than most not to take anything for granted. Life can change in an instant, and it often does.

My journey to parenthood began in April 2019 when my husband and I learned I had a very low anti-mullerian hormone (AMH) count and one functioning fallopian tube, making it difficult to conceive naturally. After multiple visits with fertility specialists, we tried intrauterine insemination (IUI), and it didn't work due to the low quality of my eggs. After that, we decided in vitro fertilization (IVF) was right for us. Through that process, we ended up with five genetically perfect embryos.

When I realized I may never conceive naturally, I felt like I was missing out on the opportunity to create life as it's meant to be created. I felt sorry for myself, but sorrier for my husband, Tim. Then I quickly stopped the self-pity. This wasn't my fault. My body wasn't incapable; it just wasn't designed how it should be. Once I made my fertility an "it is what it is" scenario, I realized I had been given the opportunity to create strength and resilience from this adversity. I told myself that when I became pregnant with the help of drugs and science, I would *still* have created life, just in a different way—and that's damn beautiful.

On November 15, 2019, we transferred two embryos into my uterus. It was a crisp, cold, and sunny day, and Tim and I both felt calm and good. During the transfer, I had Tim at my side, holding my hand; a nurse over my stomach with an ultrasound wand, moving around; my doctor in the middle; and the embryologist, controlling the embryos on a screen. It all happened in less than seven minutes. The doctor said it was "perfect," and we left the fertility clinic with a healthy amount of hope and confidence.

I could have tested at home on day seven after the transfer, but I wanted to wait an extra day. So on day eight, I woke up and took the test.

After a few minutes, we saw two lines indicating I was pregnant. I just kept saying, "Oh my God, oh my God, oh my God!" Tim held me, and I cried and cried. My only regret is that we didn't record this moment because it was so special. I would've wanted to show our raw emotions to my child one day, once they could understand. IVF is such a miraculous thing. This baby (or babies—we wouldn't know that for a few more weeks) was special already.

I finally understood why people say, "We're pregnant." It's a two-person role, especially with IVF. Tim became a master progesterone-shot administrator. He could stir up any injection "cocktail" and drove me to the train for every single blood-draw appointment.

I also now understand why every woman says the IVF journey is worth it. The power of how I felt when learning I was pregnant crushed all the tears I'd experienced that year.

Four weeks later at our first sonogram appointment in mid-December, we learned that two embryos had implanted. We were having twins! On New Year's Eve 2019, I reflected by writing in my journal:

It's the last day of the year. The last day of the decade, which everyone is making a big stink about, and I'm not sure why. Perhaps when you live in the moment every day like we do, the years and decades don't matter? I'm not so sure.

When I think about 2019, the overarching themes are positivity, gratitude, HOPE, strength, acceptance, growth, challenge, ownership, and belief.

Tim and I tried starting a family in January 2019, and when we realized we needed to enter the world of IVF, I promised myself I wouldn't let it run my life. I have been told, and have seen firsthand, how it temporarily ruins people. I allowed myself to feel all the feelings and had very dark moments but never dark days or weeks. It challenged my marriage and forced us to have discussions I wish we didn't have to have. And I'll admit that I secretly considered giving up on trying to get pregnant a few times to protect myself from emotional pain.

Fast forward to being pregnant with two babies growing inside of me; I feel almost too lucky that it all worked out how we hoped it would, knowing so many couples struggle so much more. Regardless of being pregnant or not, I LIVED in 2019. Point is, while my outcome of being pregnant is truly amazing, if I weren't pregnant, I still would've enjoyed the journey as much as I did. While 2020 will likely be much calmer in the first half as I take care of my pregnant self and am not as active around the world, the second half will be filled with a new life— as a MOM of two!!! I still haven't wrapped my head around that, but I have time. Cheers to the year 2019; it's been an awesome one. Cheers to an awesome 2020 ahead!

I still read this back to myself often, and it reminds me how fragile every moment in life is. It reminds me to embrace and enjoy every good minute, because our next minutes are not guaranteed to always be happy.

January and February 2020 were wonderful; my body was changing and growing, and I was feeling both babies move inside of me. Then the COVID-19 pandemic struck the US in March, and I continued to feel grateful about being pregnant and having the opportunity to slow life down before becoming a family of four. I had a picture-perfect appointment with my high-risk obstetrician on Friday, April 24, where the doctor said everything looked as it should for a twin pregnancy at 26.5 weeks.

The next evening, I had an awful stomachache and began vomiting. I figured it was from the Thai food that Tim and I had eaten for dinner. Although he felt fine, I was led to believe I had food poisoning because of the sharp stomach pains, hot sweats, and severe nausea. This continued for about two hours. I told Tim to go to sleep, because it was after midnight already and I didn't want to keep him up.

Then things changed, fast.

I got up from a bathroom visit and felt severe pressure in my vaginal cavity. I yelled for Tim to wake up before sitting back down on the toilet. We called the hospital and were told we'd receive a call back within thirty minutes. Meanwhile the pressure was getting worse and worse by the second. Eventually I felt like my body was about to explode.

Since we still hadn't heard from our provider, we called 911. As the operator was asking questions, something inside felt like it was dropping out of me. I reached my hand down, and a blue water-balloon-like sac came out, fully intact.

I'll never forget the look of horror on Tim's face. We thought my organs were falling out of me.

"The paramedics will be there with an ambulance between four and six minutes from now," the operator reassured. "Help is on the way."

Then I felt something else drop. I put my hands back

down toward the toilet, and I felt something more solid bulging out of me. I thought maybe my placenta was rupturing and coming out. And then I felt limbs.

"Oh my God! Oh my God! A baby!" I yelled. "It's one of the babies! A baby is out! Oh my God! Help! Please help!"

I handed the baby to Tim who was being instructed by the operator to wrap it in a clean towel. We had no idea if it was a boy or girl; neither of us even thought to check. In fact, I was still struggling to process that this was actually a baby that had come out of me. The baby was pink, whimpering like a sick kitten, and breathing. It was the smallest thing we had ever seen. When we heard the ambulance's sirens outside, it was as if God had arrived.

Tim temporarily had to leave me and the baby alone to let the paramedics into our apartment. Before he left, he laid our infant on my stomach—swaddled in the towel—and I never stopped talking to my baby, repeating, "It's OK; it's OK. We're going to be OK. Everything is going to be OK. It's OK, baby; it's OK." I wanted to sit up and see the baby's face, but my body was frozen, numb, and heavy. I couldn't move, and I didn't want to move my baby.

The paramedics told us the baby was a girl. "We need to get her out of here fast to get her hooked up to hospital machines," one of them told me.

I reminded them there was another baby inside of me.

After Tim, the baby, and I took what felt like the longest ride ever, the ambulance pulled up to the emergency entrance. My mom—who I had texted when the paramedics arrived—was standing there waiting like an angel appearing from the sky.

"Mom, I need you to accompany our daughter to the NICU so she won't be alone," I instructed while providing the medical staff with permission for her to make decisions. I trusted my mom fully, and I wanted Tim to stay with me, as it became evident I would be delivering the next baby.

After my firstborn infant was out of sight, they manually broke my water. I pushed twice and out came our baby boy. It was silent—not one cry—and I saw lots of concerned looks on every doctor's and nurse's face. They whisked him away from us and put him onto a table over my shoulder where only Tim could see, and they began aggressive resuscitation efforts. At this point, Tim and I were so fearful of our daughter not surviving, and we thought our son was our only hope for bringing any baby home.

A lady with a clipboard came into the room asking what the babies' names were. We had decided to name our son Max Mann Stevens, his first name meaning "the greatest" and his second name being my maiden name. We named our daughter Liv Haydon Stevens, her first name meaning "life" and her second name being Tim's mom's maiden name. Combined, Max and Liv meant "the greatest life," and that was our plan as first-time parents—to provide them with the greatest life possible.

At this point, Max had started breathing and was taken to the NICU to join Liv while I went into emergency surgery to remove the placentas stuck inside of me, which had broken into pieces. Throughout the births and operation, I lost an extreme amount of blood and spent the day recovering, unable to leave the bed for the next eight-plus hours to visit my babies in the NICU. No visitors were allowed due to COVID restrictions, so Tim had a very hard time getting back to me once I was out of surgery. It seemed like one long, horrible nightmare.

The NICU attending doctor came to speak with us about Max and Liv. Liv was seemingly OK, weighing a little over one pound, but the doctor explained we were nowhere near out of the woods yet. "It will be a few long months in the NICU as she learns to breathe on her own while growing," he clarified. Then he took a deep breath before adding, "Now, with Max, we are very, very, very, very, very concerned."

I looked at Tim, who had a frozen look on his face, before I asked the doctor directly: "Is Max going to die?"

He paused before responding. "We're going to do everything we can, but your son was born with multiple conditions of VACTERL syndrome, including anal atresia, tracheoesophageal fistula, esophageal atresia, and renal anomalies," he cautioned. He advised us to transfer Max to another hospital that night for emergency life-saving surgery, and we agreed. Since that hospital had superior care, we decided we wanted Liv transferred there as well; but they would wait until the next day to transfer her, since her case wasn't as acute.

It was Sunday night at this point (the babies were born earlier that morning), and Tim was required to leave due to visitor restrictions. The plan was for him to come back in the morning to be present when they transferred Liv—and hopefully discharged me from the hospital.

At around eleven p.m. that night, the new hospital called to inform me that Max had arrived safely. Around midnight, I got another call from the surgeon who was preparing him for surgery. He read me the list of risks and complications, asking for my final consent. "With this all said, understanding the potential risk and complications, do you, Alison Stevens, mother of Max Stevens, agree to this surgery?"

"Yes," I replied.

He thanked me and said he would call me again in a few hours before they began.

After hanging up the phone, I cried hysterically. I looked up and prayed to God that Max would be OK.

The surgery was delayed, as Max struggled. Then, around six a.m., I was advised they were going to begin, and that the surgery would take one and a half to two hours. In the meantime, I asked the nurse if I could go see Liv, but they wouldn't allow me due to COVID restrictions. I was so upset; how could they not allow me to walk down the hallway and see my baby girl?

My phone rang at 6:20 a.m. It was the hospital where Max was. *Please no*, I thought. *It's too soon. It's only been twenty minutes since they began. Oh God, no.* I answered the phone.

"Hi Alison, it's Dr. X."

Silence.

"I'm so sorry, but as we were getting ready to begin, Max stopped breathing. As we tried to resuscitate him, he started bleeding internally, everywhere. We tried everything; we really did. I am so sorry to tell you this, but Max has died."

I could not get any words out. I was frozen, but I knew I had to respond. "I'm here, doctor. I just need a moment, please."

"Please, please take your time."

My son was dead. He died. Gone. I no longer had my baby boy. I muted the phone and breathed loud inhales, through tears and a hysteria I'd never known before.

"OK, I'm here."

"I'm so sorry, Alison. We did everything we could."

I got out of bed and paced around the hospital room a few times, unable to catch my breath as I sobbed. I'd just had twins yesterday, and now I was alone in the hospital. My son had died, and I was forbidden to see my daughter. Was this really happening? I called Tim and woke him out of a deep sleep.

"Love, Max didn't make it. We lost him. He died."

That morning, Liv was transported to the same hospital as Max, and I was discharged in the early afternoon. As we headed to the hospital to say our goodbyes to Max and to see Liv, I felt every emotion under the sun. This is not how anything was supposed to go. I had known there was a high possibility of preterm labor with twins, but never did I think we would have only one baby after delivering two alive.

At the hospital, everyone extended their deepest condolences. They let us know Max had been kept on oxygen after he died, so his body would be warm and soft for us to hold.

He was in a private room, in a bassinet, wrapped in a swaddle with a hat on. Soft music was playing, and it was surreal and awful. I was nauseous and hot, and I asked Tim to look at him first and tell me what color he was. I needed warning.

He walked toward the bassinet, and all he could say was, "He's just beautiful. He's so beautiful."

We stood beside the bassinet together. They had placed a teddy bear next to him, and it looked like Max was sleeping. The last time we saw him, he had been hooked up to machines, wires, IVs, everything. Now he looked like a tiny, sleeping, peaceful, perfect, beautiful baby. Except there was no life inside of him. He was just a body and a soul.

I scooped him up. I needed him in my arms, and I needed to kiss him everywhere. This *need* was intense. We sat in two chairs they had placed next to the bassinet, and I asked Tim to take pictures. I knew I would want them. I had a hard time accepting the fact that this would be the last time I would hold my son. The last time I could look at him. The last time I could touch and feel him. I hated that time was limited; there's such a finite end when you're staring at death.

I kissed Max's face, his hands, and his forehead. His skin was softer than silk. I touched his lips; I touched his nose, his eyelids. I continued to kiss his face everywhere. Then I touched his lips to mine. I kept wishing I'd feel his breath, but it was empty. My tears wet his tiny, perfect face. Tim and I stared at him, not wanting to stop.

Then I handed Max to Tim. Tim kissed his face like I had, and we cried together. Tim said a prayer over Max, and we talked to him together. We apologized to him and told him we hoped so badly that he hadn't suffered in pain. We told him how much we loved him. We thanked him for giving us the opportunity to experience this type of love. We told him he would always be our firstborn son, and we would never forget him.

I can't say how long we spent with him in that room

together; time had frozen. When we felt it was time to put him back in the bassinet, we did. I stroked his face with my finger a few more times, continued to cry over him, and bent over the bassinet to give him more kisses. Then we agreed it was time to go see our baby girl in the NICU. We said goodbye to one life and knew we had to focus on saving our daughter's life. And that's what we did.

The outpouring of love and support we received from our friends, family, and coworkers was unforgettable. Receiving congratulations and condolence wishes simultaneously was something I never knew was possible. The way people showed up for us, during the peak of the COVID lockdown in New York, was really special. People set up meal trains and sent and delivered home-cooked meals, flowers, cards, paper towels, and toilet paper. They made donations in Max's memory to the NICU where he died, sent special gifts, planted trees in the babies' names, and named stars for them. Tim and I were overwhelmed in the best possible way by their thoughtful gestures and acts of kindness. To say we were humbled is an understatement.

The NICU journey was what every NICU parent says it is: an unpredictable roller coaster. For five weeks, Liv took one step forward, then three steps back. We visited her every single day, yet we struggled because we could not visit her together due to COVID restrictions. It was lonely and terrifying, and the staff seemed very bent out of shape about everything because at the time, it was six weeks post-lockdown in New York City.

Liv had suffered a bilateral brain bleed, so her brain development was one of our largest concerns. In addition to the bilateral bleeds, she experienced what most preterm babies born at 26.5 weeks experience: heart and lung developmental delays along with a host of other complications. Her doctors assured us that every NICU baby is on their own schedule and this was all normal. We advocated for Liv daily, pushed for extra testing that they said they normally wouldn't do, asked for brain ultrasounds frequently, and voiced our opinions and concerns about anything that we questioned—feeding amounts, treatments, medications, procedures, etc. Then on May 28, we got the greatest, most relieving news that her brain bleeds were beginning to resolve themselves. We were elated. We could see the light and knew we had to practice patience, as Liv needed at least another two to three months to grow in the NICU before coming home.

Just one day later, everything went downhill. We got a call in the morning that Liv had a very difficult night. Her heart rate was worrisome, she had vomited, her belly was swollen, and her bowel movements had stopped. The doctors told us they were very concerned. They stopped giving her my breast-milk and fed her through IV, and they intubated her. The doctors kept telling us, "Liv is very, very, very sick," and promised they were doing everything they could to determine what was causing this sudden decline. They continued to run test after test and assigned her a one-to-one, 24/7 nurse.

The next morning, we received a phone call requesting that we get to the hospital quickly, that Liv's condition was worsening by the minute, and we would need to have a difficult conversation when we got there. We jumped into the car, didn't speak a word, and prepared for them to tell us Liv was dying.

At the hospital, Tim and I were both allowed through the doors together. We knew things must have gotten bad because prior to today, we had only been allowed to visit one at a time. There were more than ten medical professionals in her pod, which was blocked off entirely so that no other visiting parents could see her condition. Huge oxygen tanks surrounded her, and a noisy oscillating ventilator was keeping her alive.

The attending physician approached us to tell us Liv may not make it through the next few hours. He suggested we hold her.

I bluntly asked, "Are you saying she is going to die?"

The doctor nodded. Then another doctor came towards Liv's bed and studied her condition. He was a surgeon and said he could *try* to do surgery, to open her stomach to see how damaged her intestines were and try to remove part of her bowel that was causing so much damage—but that it was super high risk.

"So, we can either hold her until she passes in our arms, or we can try surgery," I said, summarizing our options. "What would be her survival rate without surgery?"

"Less than 5 percent," the surgeon answered.

We opted for the surgery.

My parents came to keep us company in the waiting room. We knew there was a high chance that the surgeon would come out at any moment and tell us Liv hadn't made it.

She survived the surgery on Saturday, but now we needed to make it to Monday for a second operation. We knew we could lose her at any moment because she was still so sick.

The surgery was postponed for another day because Liv was too weak. Seeing our baby in this condition was crushing. She was swollen with fluids, two times her normal size. She started having seizures and got sepsis and E. coli. Her doctors told us we were hanging on for a miracle and warned us she could have severe brain damage from everything she had suffered. We opted for a brain MRI to understand her long-term outcome. The MRI showed the most severe brain damage possible. Even if she were to survive, Liv would likely have no cognitive, motor, breathing, and feeding abilities—ever.

As Liv's last days with us approached, it was torture not to be able to hold and cuddle her. Our families were allowed to visit her once, to meet her and say goodbye in the same visit.

On June 13, we held Liv as they unhooked her from her life support. We cradled her in our arms for more than forty-five minutes as we waited for her to take her last breath, and for her heart to stop. Using a stethoscope, we listened to her heart slowing and knew when the time was coming. I held her head in my neck, smelling her and kissing her. Like I'd done with Max, I put my lips onto hers. But this time, I felt her warm—albeit weak—breath. She started licking my lips; she knew I was her mom. She felt my lips on hers, and that lightened my heavy heart for a moment.

There are no words to describe the feeling of watching your baby take her last breath. At just seven weeks old, she had been with us for such a short period of time, and after this I would never see her beautiful face again. Her lips were turning blue, and I knew the time was nearing. I kept kissing her and talking to her, telling her it was OK to go to sleep. "Mommy and Daddy love you, sweet girl. And we're right here. We're right here, my love."

The doctor who had been monitoring her heart outside the room came in and told us she had passed. We held her, and each other, and cried and cried. We tucked her into bed, took more photos, and continued to kiss her until her body temperature began rapidly declining and her face changed. I didn't want to remember her like that, so I gave her my last long kiss on her delicate face. We left the NICU hand in hand, with broken hearts and empty arms. It was the darkest, most painful moment of my life. When we got into the car and turned on the radio, the song "Carry On" by Fun played. It was a sign from Liv and Max.

The months following my losses were filled with extreme emotional pain. I connected with other moms who had lost their infants, found some podcasts that helped my healing process, met with a therapist, and allowed myself to feel whatever came my way. Because of COVID, I was forced to sit with my feelings and not escape them. There was nowhere to go, nothing to do, no way to keep busy. Looking back, I realize this helped with my healing because I was forced to feel.

My goal every day was to simply get out of bed. And I

did. I was kind to myself and gave myself grace and space to cry and scream into my pillow. I went for a lot of long walks and talked silently to Liv and Max, asking them to send me signs. They did, and they still do.

Five years later, emotions from grief still crash down on me in the most unexpected times, and I know that will continue for a very, very long time. I am kind to myself, I give myself grace, and I express my needs to my husband. I do everything I can not to push the feelings aside, because I know that the long-term impact of doing that would be detrimental to my grieving process.

If you are a man or woman suffering from pregnancy loss, a miscarriage, or child loss, know that whatever and however you are feeling is right. There is no right and wrong way to grieve.

Accept the fact that not everyone will understand your feelings and your pain, and that's OK. People will say hurtful things; they do not mean it. Find space in your broken heart to forgive them; don't let additional anger build up inside of you. You already have enough from the loss.

Identify the two or three people who help you the most and talk to them as much as you can. For me, that was my mom, my husband, and another mom I was introduced to who had lost her twins and became a dear friend.

Listen to podcasts and read about grief so that you don't feel so alone, and so your feelings can be validated.

Understand and accept that you may grieve differently than your partner; the spectrum of grief is broad. When I sought to understand how Tim was grieving and wholeheartedly accepted it, our grieving became more unified and peaceful. He respected my ways and I respected his, and together we took steps forward.

If you know someone who is struggling, be there for them. Whatever the extremity of their struggle may be, whether it's dealing with the death of a loved one, a health crisis, or a loss of a job, *show up*. When everyone comes together to help someone heal, the power in numbers fills part of the void. People often ask me how I survived the first initial weeks, and I know it was from the love and support of my friends and family. If you ever question whether to do something for someone, stop thinking and just do it. Mail the card. Show up at their door. Send a text message. Call. Leave a voicemail they will listen to later. You'll never regret showing up, but you'll likely regret being absent.

In August 2020, eleven weeks after losing Liv, we learned we were pregnant again. Second to laboring and delivering Liv in our bathroom, this was the biggest surprise of my life. I'll forever consider the conception of our third baby a gift from God. And so, I began a new journey as a pregnant, grieving mom.

Pregnancy after loss is scary, exciting, overwhelming, beautiful, ugly, and it's something no one can possibly understand unless they've experienced it. I knew I had to be a brave warrior, for myself and for my baby.

I spent the first twenty-six weeks living in fear of losing another baby and filled with anxiety about experiencing another preterm birth. Once I reached twenty-six weeks and hadn't gone into labor like the first time, I was able to breathe a little. I then decided to allow my mind and heart to enjoy my pregnancy. I didn't want to later regret how I'd felt while growing a beautiful new life inside of me. So I made a conscious effort to surrender my fear and let go of the worries weighing me down. I let reality sink in, because up until this point, I hadn't faced it. I hadn't been able to picture life with a new baby, and I'd been protecting myself from history repeating itself. I mean, how could I not? At this point, however, I realized that no matter what the outcome might be, denying the new life growing within me—including both the risks and potential for joy—wouldn't protect me from anything. So for the first time, I let myself get excited.

In May 2021, we welcomed our second son into the world. We named him Teddy, which means "gift from God," and he arrived with a burst of positive energy. The birth experience was picture-perfect, with nurses and doctors surrounding us all during my labor and delivery, rooting for me as I pushed. Our son came quickly and was welcomed with cheers, high fives, laughter, and happy tears. Teddy is now four years old, healthy, thriving, and happy.

When Teddy was six months old, I was blessed with another surprise: I was pregnant again! *How could this be?* I thought. After fertility challenges, I really didn't think it was possible to get pregnant naturally, and yet I had managed to—two times?! This was another smooth pregnancy. I was exponentially calmer than the previous one after having had one successful delivery, and we welcomed our daughter, Ava, to the world in August 2022.

In 2020, I lost a son and daughter. By 2022, I had another son and daughter. Every day—quite literally when I look at Teddy and Ava in person, and Liv and Max in photos on my dresser—I hold an immense amount of gratitude in my heart. That gratitude helps me reframe any adversity that comes my way. I consider it a gift from my four children and a blessing from my hardship.

After everything, I've realized I am a proud and brave woman who's experienced infertility, egg retrievals, embryo transfers, pregnancy, traumatic preterm delivery, infant loss, grief, pregnancy after loss, and two healthy pregnancies and deliveries. I've learned that these experiences don't *define* me, but they have *redefined* my outlook and perspective on life and how I choose to live it. I am forever changed, and I consider that a gift and not a curse.

A wise and compassionate friend once told me of losing my babies, "Their having been part of you and your lives means they will forever touch and impact all those you encounter as you continue to write your life stories. You know more, see more, and love more deeply because they have been." She could not have been more right.

I'm often asked if there is any *silver lining* to everything that's happened. I'm sensitive to this term when discussing the loss of my babies, because there are no positive aspects of their deaths after having been born alive. But I can say those tragic events changed me. It's impossible for me to sweat the small stuff. My husband and I "Liv life to the Max," because we know that life can change in any given second and nothing is guaranteed. If we want to do something, we do it. If we want to go somewhere, we go. If we want to change something, we change it. We think less and do more, and that makes for a more fulfilling and rich life.

We all hold a reserve of strength deep within us, and as humans, we all have different levels of resiliency. Whatever yours may be, have faith and trust that you will survive your hardest days. We grow through what we go through, and we have a choice to overcome the obstacles that are thrown our way.

Liv life to the Max; tomorrow is not a promise, and today is a gift.

Discussion Questions

The author experienced infertility, preterm birth, and the loss of her premature twins. And while the pain and darkness she went through was excruciating, she came out of it with a new appreciation of living in the moment and seizing joy wherever it could be found.

1. The author mentions her hesitancy to talk about *silver linings* when it comes to her loss. How do you feel about this term when it comes to tragedy and hardship?
2. After experiencing such loss, the author had trouble relaxing into happiness. Have you ever felt this way? What helped you to trust in the good and live in the moment?

4

THROUGH CONCRETE

JUANA PFADT

G rabbing the test from the shelf that day, I had a heavy feeling in my stomach. It was both the anticipation of a positive result but also the sense of bracing myself for yet another disappointment. While I was walking to the register, I thought about the last time my partner and I had had sex. Somewhat defeated by peeing on ovulation strips for the past several months with no results, we had not used them during my last cycle. I was sure there was no way we had gotten the timing right, and besides, I was only two days late.

But back at home, the second line was visible within an instant. I stared at those two lines in disbelief. I was going to be a mom. We were going to be parents. After taking a second test, I sat down on the bed and took a deep breath. *Positive.* I was indeed pregnant.

The first few days of my pregnancy were peaceful. My partner had left for a business trip a week prior to me taking the test and wouldn't be back for another month. We celebrated over FaceTime when I shared the big news. I was overwhelmed by a feeling of love and gratitude. I was glowing.

There is nothing quite like the feeling of finding out you're pregnant. I wanted to shout from the rooftops and share my joy with the world. However, I felt protective of the gift I was carrying and only told my closest family members and friends in Germany that I was expecting. I could hear their smiles and happiness through the phone. It was finally happening for me.

But after two days of bliss, things suddenly changed. I went to the bathroom, and there it was. Pink, fresh blood. My heart stopped for a moment, and I tried to quell the racing thoughts that made a rational assessment almost impossible. Was I losing the baby?

After a few hours of online research, I had calmed myself enough to call my mom and best friend. This was completely normal for some women. Light pink discharge was no reason to worry unless accompanied by cramping. Everyone was in agreement that I shouldn't be too concerned. The plan was to monitor and wait.

But a few days later came the cramping. First very slightly but then growing more and more intense. So intense that I called my gynecologist.

The confusion began when I arrived at the doctor's office and was brought into the ultrasound room. The ultrasound tech was uneasy, double-checking her work and asking me repeatedly if I was sure my test was positive. I had taken eight tests by then; yes, I was sure. There was a lot of awkward silence as she stared at the screen and moved the wand inside of me. With every passing minute, I became more uneasy. Something wasn't right. My uterus was empty.

Finally talking to the doctor did nothing to reassure me. "Your urine sample confirms that you're pregnant, but the pregnancy should already be visible in your uterus, which it isn't," the physician told me. "It's possible you're experiencing an ectopic pregnancy, but I can't say for certain. You need to go home and monitor your symptoms. If the pain or bleeding gets worse, go to the emergency room."

The doctor rattled off some more information about the seriousness of ectopic pregnancies and how I could die should my tube rupture. Then they offered me the ultrasound picture of my non-viable pregnancy. I declined.

I stayed home for the weekend. But by Monday morning, the cramping had gotten worse, and I was in a lot of pain. I called the doctor again and was told to go to the hospital right away.

The emergency room was busy, and it took what felt like an eternity to get into a treatment room. The ultrasound nurse was gentle and tried to walk me through every movement. There was a bit of small talk—polite exchanges of shallow pleasantries. Then, after waiting yet another eternity for a doctor, my ectopic pregnancy was confirmed. My baby had gotten stuck in my right fallopian tube and would not survive. And neither would I if we did not kill the "cells."

I was given the option of having my fallopian tube surgically removed or taking a dosage of methotrexate, a drug commonly used in chemotherapy that would stop the cells from growing. The pregnancy—or my baby, as I was already thinking of it—would then be absorbed back into my body in four to six weeks.

After an emotional call with my partner, we decided to choose the method that would give me the highest chance of getting pregnant again. The resident assigned to me was somewhat unsure about percentages of expected fertility after each treatment and promised to get more information. She never did, and after an extensive Google search of my own, I made a decision: methotrexate.

I waited almost another two hours for someone to administer the dosage to me. While I was lying in the hospital room, waiting for the drug that would kill my baby, I received an email from my best friend. I swallowed hard and took a deep breath. I had just been invited to plan her baby shower.

A wave of confusing thoughts flooded my system. *Be happy for her, Juana. Be happy!* And I was, but I was equally jealous.

Realizing this sent me into a spiral of shame. Just one

week after one of the highest highs I had ever experienced, I was lying in a hospital bed, waiting for a shot that would kill my baby, feeling jealous of the baby my best friend was going to have. I was all alone, I was afraid, I was devastated, I was confused. Yet I found I couldn't cry.

When I spoke to my partner, he had offered to fly home. I declined, and he seemed relieved, the wedge already driven between us.

The methotrexate arrived in a sealed bag with a radioactive logo on it. The doctor joked about it, but I couldn't force even a glimmer of a smile. To me, the logo meant death. The feeling of the needle piercing my skin during the injection made my stomach turn.

The memory of the drive home from the emergency room is blurred by the emotional and physical pain I felt. Yet when I finally arrived home, my dog, Tyson—who I called "T"—was waiting to be let out after hours of being cooped up while I was at the hospital. I was bleeding pretty significantly by then, but with no pads at home, I shoved toilet paper into my panties and numbly carried out my responsibilities.

After walking T, I went straight to bed. I didn't know what to feel. Then, lying in bed, the wall I had successfully held up in the hospital came crashing down. I cried for hours. I called my partner, but the few minutes he had to spare while at work did nearly nothing to calm my fear and anxiety.

I was afraid to fall asleep all by myself and found myself typing up my will on my phone. I was afraid of dying alone in my bed. I had never thought about dying before, but with the pain growing more and more intense, I did then.

The doctor had said that if the pain got any worse, I should come back. The pain was worse, but how much worse would be bad enough to actually go back? Why did I not know what to do? Would I possibly fall asleep and not wake up? When would my partner figure out I had passed? Would he come home? Would my friends come look for me? Would

T be OK? I thought about my mom. Normally I would call her for emotional support, but it was in the middle of the night in Germany and I did not want to worry her.

The next few hours were without a doubt the loneliest of my life. The physical and emotional pain I endured that night was excruciating and all-encompassing. I had no one to comfort me, no one to hold me and reassure me I was going to be OK. Every wave of pain reminded me of the decision I'd made to kill my baby in order to survive. I hated my body. I felt guilty and selfish. I was a murderer. I had wished for this baby for so long, and now I was killing it.

For the next few days, I existed in a haze, constantly exhausted and consumed by a deep sadness. One of my best friends stopped by, but with my partner still away for work, I was mostly alone. I spent most of my time in painful darkness. Despite it being summer in Chicago, I only moved off the couch to walk T and then lay back down. Behind closed blinds, I cried and wished summer would end. I didn't want to be reminded of the happiness a Chicago summer normally brought me. I needed to be sad. Deep shadows of sorrows were marking my face. There were tears that never dried, thoughts that never stopped, and my heart physically hurt.

I used the little energy l had left to do the bare minimum of work I must do. During the first couple of days after my methotrexate injection, I found myself standing at my kitchen counter, putting together documents for my clients that had to be sent out while bleeding into a pad. Parts of my baby were leaving my body, yet I wasn't given the space to properly mourn the loss. I worked every day for the entire four weeks of my treatment, driving myself to constant lab visits to get my blood drawn while simultaneously attempting to keep my sanity.

My breakdowns were frequent. Triggered by the sunshine while walking T, sudden cramps, or my breasts reminding me that they were gearing up to nurture a baby, sometimes I couldn't bring myself to take another step. T and I would sit on the sidewalk, where I would cry until I was ready to pick myself back up and walk home. I don't know if anyone in my neighborhood saw me, but I also didn't care. Back on the couch, I would return to the darkness and loneliness that had become my reality. I longed for my family, my best friends, my partner. I longed for the touch of a loved one.

In the days and weeks following my diagnosis, I had to get my hormone levels checked every few days to guarantee that the methotrexate was working and my pregnancy levels were decreasing as desired. They weren't. That Sunday night when I received a call, I knew it wasn't a good sign. The doctor informed me that my levels were rising again and that I had to go back the next day for a second round of methotrexate. I couldn't help thinking that my baby was fighting to stay alive. Or the "cells," as my doctor so nonchalantly put it.

"We will call you tomorrow morning to let you know next steps, but you have to come back in tomorrow," the doctor said. I cried all night, trying to make sense of what was happening to me, but I simply couldn't.

The next morning came and nobody called. By noon, I called the office and explained my situation. Deer in head-lights. Nobody knew what was going on. A nurse promised to get back to me after finding out more information. She did call me back a couple of hours later and explained that I would have to go to the emergency room, as my doctor had failed to put in an order for the methotrexate at the only outpatient facility authorized to administer such a heavy drug. Which explained why nobody reached out to me in the morning—my doctor had simply forgotten about me.

Exhausted and defeated, I returned to the emergency room and waited for two hours. The doctor entered the exam room with a familiar looking bag marked with the bright radioactive logo that will forever be burned into my memory. I felt like I was standing in the corner, looking at myself lying on the bed. This time, I didn't flinch when the needle entered my body.

A week after my second dosage, I finally stopped bleeding and my levels decreased. Each time I went back to the office to get my blood drawn, the numbers were lower and lower. Then on September 4, 2019, I finally saw it in black and white: *zero*. My baby was dead.

Seeing the number, I wondered if this was the moment to feel happy again. Should I be relieved? Should I be sad? Was I allowed to be both? While I was left in emotional limbo trying to figure out what to feel, my body was quite sure which route to take. My breasts started to relax and become softer again, and only eleven days after my last visit to the lab, my period arrived. My body was healing itself, and my soul didn't know how to catch up. Looking in the mirror, I began to look more like myself again, but from the inside I felt so different.

My partner had returned home by now, but things between us were off. We tiptoed around each other, hiding our feelings from each other as best we could. We never talked about what happened. Never cried together. Never held each other. Never acknowledged each other's pain.

We moved to Arizona for a new job he'd been offered, but in the end, after living together like two heartbroken strangers for six months, we broke up. He couldn't deal with my pain, and I wasn't able to accept that he seemed so indifferent about everything. The very moment I stepped into that hospital room, the end of our relationship had manifested itself.

After the breakup, T and I moved back to Chicago. Within a week of our arrival, the city went into a two-month shutdown. COVID had taken over the world, and I found myself confined to my one-bedroom apartment. There was no escaping the lonely hours of isolation and the constant thoughts that flooded my mind. I relived the loss of my baby, the separation from my family and friends, and the end of my relationship in a million different ways.

Riddled with pain, I felt so many conflicting and complex emotions. I felt guilty for trying to move on, guilty for feeling guilty, and guilty for not feeling guilty enough. I felt that it was my fault I had lost my baby. I pondered over and over how different my life could have been had I made different choices along the way. I wondered if my ex and I would still be together had I not lost the baby, if my body had functioned the way it should have instead of failing.

It was excruciating, but for the first time in my life, I let myself feel and experience the loss without distracting myself. No dating, no get-togethers with friends, no parties, no bars. Just me and the past. While the world as we knew it was falling apart around me, I began to fall into place. Quarantine, as strange as that may sound, was my savior and maybe my biggest blessing in disguise. I overcame my pain by moving through it. By acknowledging its existence—its validity—and allowing the complexity of its nuances to guide me through my grieving process.

It wasn't only the loss of my baby that had left me para-lyzed, but also the loss of my identity. Somehow, I had put so much importance on becoming a mother that I had forgotten to see myself as complete. I had put all my eggs in one basket, and once that basket was completely empty, so was I.

Once I surrendered to the pain, though, it became bear-able. I realized that welcoming the future and slowly letting go of the pain does not erase the past or mean you forget it. Once I embodied that concept, I started to heal. I began to allow joy back into my life, and hope followed shortly there-after. Learning to live in the present moment, without over-whelming myself with thoughts of the past or future, was the true catalyst for change. I found myself smiling at the sun or giggling if T did something goofy. I started to sing in the shower again and enjoy the feeling of water caressing my body. A body that wasn't the same anymore, marked with invisible scars of my painful journey, but a body still perfect.

I sometimes feel just a hint of jealousy when I look at my best friends who have babies or toddlers. The "I'm pregnant" call never gets easier. I love my best friends dearly, but I cannot shake the occasional feeling of envy as I navigate my childless life. Being kind to myself in that regard has been a learning process.

I often have feelings of jealousy, guilt, sadness, joy, disconnect, love, hope, and faith—sometimes all at the same time. But when it comes to overcoming loss, there is no handbook for the "right" emotions, and there is also no timeline for when it is appropriate to feel them. My healing journey is continuous, and I am patiently traveling down the path of forgiving myself for all that has happened. A path of accepting the past and allowing the future to unfold.

My journey has forced me to peel back all layers of my soul in a vulnerable dance where everyone seems to be watching and judging me. I can be told how to move my body, but in the end, the only person able to execute the moves is me. No matter how good or well-intentioned the advice is, I am the one who needs to learn how to bend my body, find rhythm, and become in-sync with the song that is my life.

Most importantly, I must let go of other people's expectations of me. Their dance and their speed do not need to be mine. I can admit that I'm still perfecting my dance moves. Sometimes I'm on the beat, and sometimes I'm not. Sometimes I feel defeated and tired. But most of the time, even when hopelessness sets back in, I have faith. Faith for all the good things this life has to offer me. A cumulation of light that always welcomes me whenever I'm ready to step out of the darkness.

I haven't given up on my wish to become a mother, but I've also accepted that motherhood may or may not find me. I've also accepted that even if it finds me, it might not be the way I envisioned it when I was younger.

Life creates an abundance of opportunities for us. And

while not all of them will bring the outcomes we wish for, they are all an ongoing chance to evolve, learn, and grow. Every setback, every loss, and every detour creates room for something else that can develop in its place. And each new opportunity creates hope, reassuring me that there will always be a tomorrow.

I believe there are no limits to what my life can be. And while I don't know whether I will ever carry a child of my own or welcome one into my life, I find solace in knowing that joy, happiness, and hope will always be part of me, even if children are not in my future. I find hope in a beautiful sunrise. In the way my skin is touched by the sun for the first time after a long Chicago winter. In the embrace of someone I love. In conversations with my mother and evenings spent with good friends. I find hope in T, who is unapologetically happy every day on walks through nature, where I am so often amazed by the creation of life. I find hope in myself, and in the resilience that my body and mind have shown me over the past two years.

My life has never followed a linear path. And for too long, I've tried to live a life defined by a vision of what I thought it should be. In doing so, I have often gotten in the way of being present in the moment and accepting the natural ups and downs on my journey. Only in loss was I fully able to accept that the reality of my life will, without a doubt, deviate from the expectations I set for myself. And one thing is sure: Regardless of what cards life deals me, I will play my best game.

To my beloved baby: You were loved long before you were conceived. You are loved today and always will be.

Discussion Questions

The author writes about how she was forced to terminate an ectopic pregnancy to save her own life and how alone she felt in doing so. She wasn't able to fully heal until COVID forced her into isolation, where she had no distractions from her feelings and instead began to process them. Ultimately this healing gave her hope for the future and an understanding of how to find joy even in the darkness.

1. The author describes feeling alone while navigating the end of her pregnancy. She didn't know how to share her feelings with her friends and partner. What do you think keeps us from reaching out for help from others or holding more open conversations about pregnancy loss? How can we change this dynamic so we can speak more freely and thereby process our feelings?

2. The author shares how her life hasn't followed a linear path, and how it was only through letting go of the expectations of herself and others that she could heal. Have you ever felt hemmed in by similar expectations? How did your life change when you were able to let them go?

5

CHILD-FREE BY CHOICE: HOPEFUL RUMINATIONS

CHRISTINE NGUYEN

"I actually like children. Truly."

I've had to say this phrase numerous times over the past couple of decades as the well-meaning people around me notice that I am, curiously, a woman approaching a certain age with no small humans in tow. Had I been given a dollar for every time I have uttered this justification for my child-free existence—couched in awkward, somewhat self-deprecating laughter—I would probably now be the owner of a huge Versailles-like estate that houses all the street dogs of many nations.

As I type this, I'm perched on the edge of my chair, with a small rescue terrier fast asleep in the much more comfortable part of the seat behind my bottom. I am a Vietnamese-Australian female who recently passed the "Big 4-0." Being an only child, I always longed for siblings. However, despite having quite a sheltered childhood and adolescence (read: *hyper-protective mother*), I was rarely bored, as books and art supplies filled my days and kept my New Kids on the Block–obsessed brain busy. Ah, the days before endless device-scrolling.

Looking back, I never role-played being a mother to dolls

like I remember my friends doing. It never occurred to me. My Barbie dolls were always in their high heels—working, driving my friend's highly coveted Barbie convertible, or going out dancing with Ken in their fancy Dream Glow ball gowns. The heady eighties. Looking back, I can say with certainty that I never engaged in or felt anything that vaguely resembled maternal or motherly aspirations.

I watched TV shows like *The Brady Bunch*, *Neighbours*, and *Bewitched*, which all depicted traditional ideas of "normal" family life. Yet they looked nothing like my own experience. As is common with many Asian immigrant families, I was always surrounded by extended family members—grandparents, uncles, aunties, cousins, and close family friends. My parents divorced when I was twelve. As a result, my mother and I evolved into more of a cohabitants' arrangement than your stereotypical mother-daughter relationship. Our frank discussions about sex, school, friends, future options, and plans imparted in me the ability to recognize that I did *not* have to pursue any path that did not align with who I was or what I wanted. Although we had (and still have) a somewhat tumultuous relationship, and have fought about everything under the sun, the most valuable benefit of having such an unorthodox understanding with my forward-thinking mother is that not once have I ever felt pressure from within my own immediate family to pursue motherhood.

Let me tell you now that this is quite rare within Asian families. Unicorn-rare. I reflect back now and am deeply grateful for this space throughout the years following my teens when, on occasion, I grappled internally with these societal expectations that women explicitly and implicitly face. These days, as an English as a foreign language (EFL) teacher in Asia, I regularly find myself discussing similar issues with my female students. I am placed in an almost confessional situation, as these young women wrestle these age-old familial and societal pressures to "do their feminine duty." More on that later.

You Need Children—The Twenties and Thirties

In my early twenties, I met my partner, Dennis (aka, Den). It's sometimes unbelievable that we are still together today, and even more so that we still find each other equally hysterical. However, I am the funnier one. By a long shot. But, we are each other's best friend, and I am grateful to witness with him the wonderful, absurd (and occasionally turbulent) daily chaos in which we consistently find ourselves.

Neither of us had any interest in "settling down," despite all the weddings and baby showers we suddenly found ourselves attending. However, something did click for us in our own way because around this time, Den and I decided to get "serious." For us, though, this meant we both went back to university to finish getting qualified in our respective fields, and we moved into our "pretending-to-adult" phase.

This world of early adulting is where the polite inquiries about my childbearing plans started to seep into conversations. Whereas discussions once centered around the hippest restaurants to try, Wes Anderson films to gush over, or recent off-the-beaten-track holiday trips we'd taken, suddenly I could not seem to escape the slow creep of children-related questions from colleagues, friends, extended family, and random acquaintances. As a woman, I felt like I suddenly had a neon sign above my head with my age on it at a town hall meeting where all the agenda items were to ask me about my uterus and its five-year strategic plan.

"When are you thinking of having your first …?"

("… Coffee? Not sure, 'cause I'm already on my third for the day.")

"Do you want a boy or a girl?"

("I'm not too fussed. I've never met a dog I didn't like.")

"Will you keep working if you have a kid?"

("Well, I suppose I would need downtime.")

I know that these are all caring, well-intentioned, concerned inquiries that folks bring up when the common topics of family, work, and future plans arise during socializing. However, I always felt uncomfortable and thrown off whenever the subject of kids and family plans came up. My responses usually consisted of me making some vague and generic response about "traveling first" or "yeah, we're thinking about it." Truth be told, *we* were not thinking about it at all. And I *definitely* was not thinking about it.

I reached a point where I started to dread work gatherings, family get-togethers, or meeting new people because inevitably I would find myself fielding intrusive personal questions. There were so many other topics I found fascinating and would rather talk about. So I did not understand why, despite my obvious disinterest, others always circled back to asking me about having children.

In preparing to attend events, I would get preemptively bored and slightly anxious while anticipating the earnest insistence that I "would be such a fun mum," that I'd "love having kids!" and that I "wouldn't know love until I had a child." I will come back to that last one. I wasn't alone though, and through all these mingling events, Den was tackling his own male variations of such questions. Let it be known, however, that I am competitive. And though it's not about winning, I was definitely getting the bulk of the procreation inquiries.

During this period, we would both come away from these social gatherings a bit incredulous and bewildered that others were so curious about our "no-thoughts-of-babies" stance and lifestyle. Not only curious, but increasingly and fervently adamant that we would change our minds eventually. At this point, Den and I had probably been together for close to a decade, yet we had never gone out of our way to formally discuss having children. Rescuing more dogs, sure. But kids? You could say that bringing more lives into the world was not high on either of our individual or joint priority lists. So we had never really felt the need to talk about it.

These increasingly awkward social events, however, forced our hand. So one day, like the responsible adults we were, we sat down to explicitly address the matter. Not to simplify or trivialize the importance of the conversation that was had that day, but it basically went like this:

Me: "Do you want kids, love? I think we should decide because I'm getting a bit tired of the questions."

Dennis: "To be honest, I hadn't really thought about it, but if we need to decide now, then probably ... not really? Why? Do you?!"

Me: (Huge internal sigh of relief) "Oh, thank *gawd*. Same. Not really. It's not something that I really want to happen. Does that make me weird?! Are we weird?!"

And that was the crux of it. Unlike so many of our peers around us, neither of us had that deep gnawing desire to create mini versions of ourselves. We felt complete as we were and did not feel it was fair to bring a child into the world when both potential parents were a bit ambivalent about the whole thing. That is not to say that if it accidentally happened, we would not have loved our child—far from it. But given that we were in a position to choose, we chose the ride with no kids on it. We were both appreciative of our lives as they were. We liked, loved, and respected each other. We relished the time spent together and apart. We had a rescue dog named Digger, with a myriad of issues, who we both doted on. Both of us had work that was challenging, yet we ensured our dog had all the creature comforts. We traveled regularly to far-flung dots on the map when we felt like it. And we both had our own individual interests as well as shared interests. In short, neither of us felt that there was anything at all missing from our lives.

Post-Decision

After this hallelujah, stance-confirming chat with Den, I felt as if a mental weight had suddenly lifted. Up until that point, I had been feeling embarrassed and perhaps slightly ashamed that I didn't feel nor understand this society-mandated feminine desire of wanting children. Subconsciously, I believe I had internalized the fear that there might be something wrong with me as a woman—that something was not quite whole within me. I had experienced numerous moments of envy, when I would feel alien-like in the company of female friends who could do those baby-cooing noises so effortlessly and make the joyful gush over newborns look deliriously natural. Where were these instincts in me? I had no clue how to act in the presence of these milk-scented tiny humans with their doting adults, so I would copy my fellow females to appear normal while hoping that my mimicry didn't come off stilted or disingenuous. Because it wasn't. Please don't get me wrong; I was genuinely happy for my newly-minted parental friends. But I always felt like I was somehow tainting this precious milestone moment of theirs with my female-impostor syndrome and lack of baby-ness.

However, these self-diminishing feelings parted and dissipated like clouds after my chat with Dennis that day. During those early days of trying to settle into and cement my child-free stance in my own mind, I was hyperaware of not coming off as being anti-children or as judging those who wanted and chose to have children. I watched and cheered from the child-free seats as girlfriends around me were either embracing the sleepless early throes of motherhood or planning to get there. I made cups of tea, offered hugs, squeezed hands, and lent ears to listen to my dear friends struggling to conceive. There was so much joy in those days, yet sometimes also deep and racking heartbreak. I couldn't help but be in utter awe of this immense bravery in my friends for choosing to undertake what

I perceived to be such an enormous responsibility. Wanting to usher another entire human being into this world? Being responsible and accountable for so much of how this new person engages with and perceives the world we live in? Huge kudos to all the parents out there putting their all into their kids and trying to raise decent human beings.

Coming back to what I said at the start, I actually really like children. I find them funny, imaginative, creative, and, a lot of the time, I enjoy hanging out with them more than adult company. There's also usually a shared interest in dinosaurs and building cubby forts. I like them—I just don't want any to call my very own. I greatly enjoy and adore my role as "Aunty Chris" to my nieces and nephews and best friends' little ones. I revel in spoiling them, plying them with sugar, and then returning them to their parents (sorry, not sorry).

There is a little voice inside my head, though, that does occasionally pipe up when I'm sharing an "awwmygosh, they're so cute—this is so fun!" moment with any of my nieces or nephews.

Little internal voice: *So do you want them yet? How does this feel? Could you imagine one of your own? Look at her wittle shoes with hearts on them!*

So far, despite the doe eyes and onslaught of giggly cuteness, the answers to the above have always remained a resolute, *No, Brain. It's OK. It's fun but I'm good. Thanks for asking.*

It's like an internal temperature check—my inner you're-a-faux-woman gremlin that is still clinging to seeds of doubt and the cautionary words of clucky girlfriends from eons ago:

"Oh, trust me; you'll want them someday."

"I was like you. I didn't want them either, and then *wham,* I suddenly wanted them!"

A tiny part of me still questioned if I was "normal"—whether we had made the right choice. However, those internal, conflicted moments were becoming increasingly rare. I was more hopeful that, in choosing to be child-free, space and time in my life could be filled with my own versions of grand endeavors and adventures that would silence the nagging doubts once and for all.

What Came Next: Australia, Africa, Asia

Which brings me to the plot twist. In 2014, after a decent few years working long hours, being duly compensated for doing so, and living a textbook, comfortable life in Australia, Dennis, Digger, and I moved to Tanzania, and then finally landed in Myanmar. Although children were not the missing element in our lives, something else was. And the call to shake something up had been getting increasingly louder, as we were both grinding through our days and living to make it to the week-end. Occasionally, Dennis and I had talked about wanting to contribute and experience more—helping those who had not found the same opportunities that we both had. I can't remember the exact moment now, but eventually the wistful talking got boring. So we looked each other square in the eye, laughed at the absurdity of what we were about to embark on, and bit the bullet. We quit our jobs, donated or sold everything that we couldn't carry on our backs, and packed up our dog's belongings to head out and see what we could offer the world.

And that's how we found ourselves heading up to northern and extremely rural Myanmar, where a close friend of ours had been teaching English to internally displaced persons (IDPs) along the Thai/Myanmar border. Our friend had iden-tified a need for education provision in the rural provinces, so we all put our heads together and decided to open an English and social sciences learning center called DevelopEd (Devel-opment and Education) in a small town called Lashio in Northern Shan State. This would allow us to give rural communities access to quality education.

The Lashio learning center was a two-story house, nestled in a local neighborhood, that we converted into classrooms and space to house twelve to sixteen boarding students plus us teachers upstairs. Our students were rural youth—young men and women in their late teens to early twenties who did not have the means (financial or otherwise) to leave their communities and study in the bigger cities. What they and their communities did desire was to learn about international subjects and topics not taught or even offered in the local schools. Subjects as diverse as world history, geography, human biology (without skipping the reproduction-related chapters), gender studies, politics, and the like. And of course, all were taught in English, as our Burmese language skills were very rudimentary in those early days.

We had arrived in Myanmar at a time when the country was still slowly waking up from decades of military rule and being closed off from the rest of the world and the international community. As we became familiar faces around the place, people were shy and hopeful, but caution colored every conversation and interaction. Despite this, people were extremely friendly and welcoming—eager to meet and chat to these weird foreigners who had suddenly popped up in their town. Myanmar people are some of the kindest, most helpful, and most generous people I have ever met. As we were slowly adopted into the community, we were treated to the best of local cooking—almost daily, as neighbors would bring around dishes that they had prepared, fretting that we weren't eating properly. The extended family—our students and their parents—would drop off parcels of street snacks or fruit. Local friends would see me walking to the shops and tell me to hop on the backs of their bikes, and I'd find myself whisked off for an impromptu bowl of noodles at "the best noodle shop in Lashio, Chris!" (Note: Everyone had a different "best noodle shop," and that was OK with me—they were all world-class.) Post-noodles, I'd be dropped off at the shop that I had initially been walking to so I could complete my errand. The language of love and care here was food.

A close second extension of this all-embracing care came via comments on my personal appearance from the young women in my classes. I had arrived in Myanmar with my hair shaved close to the scalp, as was the common style for women in Tanzania. However, suddenly my coconut-head was regarded as an oddity. I received quizzical looks and timid questions about why I had short hair:

"Are you sick, Chris?"

"You would look more beautiful with long hair."

"It makes you look like a boy, *naw*?"

And so on.

Myanmar females, it turns out, take pride in—and attach significant status to—maintaining their glossy waterfalls of long black tresses. It's seen as very feminine. In fact, it's even a marital status indicator within some ethnic groups; young women will grow their hair out for as long as they are unwed. Only once married will they chop the locks to a more manageable length. The marriageable age for young women was also generally lower than in Western societies. Out in the villages, girls as young as fourteen or fifteen were getting married to start families. Given this cultural context, my hair —coupled with my age, unmarried status, and lack of chil-dren—was a frequent source of curiosity.

While I felt my femininity questioned again—yet from a different angle—I simultaneously felt secure enough within myself, deeply touched, and privileged that I was trusted enough to be included in such conversations with these inquis-itive young women. Girls in their late teens and early twenties who were starting to feel that familial and societal push to "find a good man, get married, continue the generations" (that's verbatim, by the way). Girls who were, as the outside world began seeping into Myanmar, starting to realize they might have options other than playing supporting roles to male bosses, boyfriends, or future husbands.

We would hold open-question sessions in class where I would ask the students what their dream jobs would be—no limitations, no thoughts of having studied for the right qualifications, no financial considerations. Early on in my time in Lashio, I distinctly remember that these sessions would reveal the unseen boundaries that young females and their innate capabilities existed within. Societal and familial constraints, warnings—whether spoken or internalized from those around them—about what females could and should do (and more often, "shouldn't do").

When it came to answering such a harmless question about their dreams, these young girls—often at the top of their classes academically—would give my question a fair bit of thought, and then finally proclaim that they wanted to be a CEO's assistant or secretary. *Maybe* an airline stewardess. Or a senior ticket seller at one of the local bus companies.

When I'd gently ask them, "Could you be the CEO?" or "What if you *owned* the bus company?" I'd see the light bulbs flicker on behind their eyes as their dream shifted and unexpectedly expanded. Chatting casually to these girls in the slow wind-down of class afterwards, they tell me that they'd never really been asked what they wanted to do, what dreams or ambitions they had.

I treaded cautiously in those early days as I got to know my students, their lives, and my new surroundings. It felt like a different world and era. With every conversation came newfound appreciation and gratitude for every step that had led me to these earnest and confidante-like chats under the lychee trees lining our school's compound. I listened with hope to their dreams, marveled at the differences between our lived experiences and known worlds, and giggled with them as we compared the similarities in Asian families the world over. (For example, mothers will always be mothers, no matter how old their children are!) I shared my own experiences and challenges, offered some advice and a shoulder to cry on when needed, and always took care not to be seen as challenging their family's plans for them. Many a time, students would comment that they didn't know anyone my age—female or male—who they could talk to this openly about their thoughts, hopes, misgivings over life in general, and goals. This was understandable, given how hierarchical and gendered Myanmar culture is. To be entrusted with such vulnerability was, and still is, incredibly precious to me.

The seasons changed from scorching hot months with no water in our wells to the rainy season with monsoonal storms for weeks on end. And I, too, experienced subtle changes within myself as I slowly came to love and care for these students. I felt protective of them as I imagined I would have of my own children, were that ever to be a thing in this life (still a hard pass). This was a natural evolution, given we all lived 24/7 in each other's pockets—learning, living, cooking, cleaning, fighting, celebrating, attending family weddings and funerals, and adopting neighborhood dogs together. Without realizing it had even happened, my previously quite fervent no-children stance had slowly taken a turn to *well, I guess this is my version of quasi-motherhood—and I kinda like it.* It's surreal to think that all it took was two continent shifts and a move to middle-of-nowhere Myanmar to discover my own unique definition and experience of "mothering."

At first, whenever any of the students likened me to their mothers or called me their "mother-hen," I'd find myself internally bristling. *What?! Me?! A non-mother?!* But over time, I realized and came to appreciate these comments for the meaningful gifts that they were, given to me with guileless affection and gratitude—all the more precious, given that many of my students who were studying and boarding with us were so far away from their own loving and adored mothers back in their villages. Perhaps it was because I was the loudest and most persistent about reminding them to clean their plates or put on sunscreen if they were heading out. Or maybe it was because of the help I offered them in the kitchen if they were on cooking duty, or the quiet chats, or the shoulder hugs if they looked a bit down. Whatever it was, this had become a joyful responsibility that I quietly cherished and adored.

My days and eventually years in Northern Shan State saw many class groups come and go. And although I have worked with a wide range of students during my years in Lashio and later in lower Myanmar, the most impactful and meaningful experiences that I continue to carry in my head and heart are the intimate, informal, outside-of-class/work-time chats I have shared with my female students and work colleagues. Coming back to a previous point where I had been told often that I *wouldn't know love until I had a child,* this here—being able to support and guide these women—was my chosen flavor of that love. Being able to provide a safe space for my girls—I say "girls," but some were also close to my age—to ask questions they were too embarrassed or ashamed to ask anyone else. Being their go-to "older" sister who wouldn't tell their mothers —or other sisters for that matter—what we talked about.

In some of my classes, I had teachers—female professors and lecturers who I would consider my peers or as older sisters —all whip-smart, motivated, multiple degree and PhD holders dedicated to their chosen career paths as educators. In other classes, I'd be working with international non-governmental organizations (INGO) coordinators, engineers, or logistics managers in charge of large state-wide teams. Yet all these women felt "tainted"—yes again, a literal expression they used to describe themselves—because for whatever reason, they were single and childless and somehow didn't feel quite successful or *whole* in the eyes of Myanmar society. The shades of this I had felt in my own life back in Australia were amplified a hundred times over for them.

I would often reiterate with *all* my students and staff that no subject was taboo, no question too silly—English-related or otherwise. This vulnerability is not questioned much in Western societies, but in cloistered and rigorously hierarchical rural Myanmar, it's counterintuitive in traditional classrooms, let alone with a person you regard as your senior. And so, the torrent of questions about sex, all things period-related, farts, and masturbation flowed, as did the nervous and hilarious follow-up giggles—sometimes in all-girl groups, occasionally in mixed groups. Hesitant and shy initially, the girls (especially) would make my heart burst with internal yay when they eased into asking whatever came to their minds. Being able to normalize these topics for these women—young and older—and provide clarity and factual answers to some of these questions about "things I heard from my cousin about, *you know*" was an unexpected yet rewarding part of my role in these women's lives.

With my teenage students, especially, I was a supportive ear to listen to their very private and closely guarded thoughts about not actually wanting to get married or have kids— voices normally boisterous and joyful yet literally lowered down to almost whispers with the guilt of seemingly going against their families, society, and culture itself. Whatever my students' individual circumstances, though, all I hoped to demonstrate to these glorious women was that there were always alternatives—options and hope no matter what society or their families told them. Cultural and social pressures exist within all our societies.

Listening to Yourself

Throughout our chats and time together, it was and is my hope that I have given them seeds of courage to absorb what works for them and do what makes them happy, be that pursuing a family or otherwise. I hope I have enabled each of my students to listen to their own voice, the tiny one inside their head and heart that can often be drowned out by the din of those who are well-meaning or the internalized notions of what others think is best.

It is my hope that in sharing my story, it will offer you comfort and confidence in knowing there are always alternatives and options in your life. This is for anyone—women and men, younger or older—currently doubting or second-guessing their choices or struggling to determine the way forward. No matter how set in stone a situation may feel, there are always other options.

I chose to listen really hard, straining almost, to hear my internal voice. Together, that voice and I made some pretty random choices. Correct or otherwise, each decision fit me and my life at the time when I made it. Did I have doubts then? Sure. Do I have regrets now? Not really. Would I have done some things differently? Sure, but don't we all have those wishes? Regardless of whether the decision was to start a family or not, to pursue a new career, or something seemingly as inconsequential as ordering a different coffee than usual, every misstep, success, and hair-brained scheme has led me to this moment.

I've learned that sometimes options present themselves in an obvious manner, and other times you might need to skip continents and hunt for opportunities in the backwaters of nowhere. Just go forward in *your* life as you see fit. It is *yours* to make the most of, *yours* to enjoy as you live through it.

Finally, for the female readers out there, please feel comfort in knowing there are a myriad of other possibilities beyond getting married, supporting your partner, being someone's "other half"—note that you're whole as you are!—or having kids. If you believe that getting married and raising a family will make you happy, then do that! Or is filling a house with exotic indoor plants and leopard-print chaise lounges your thing? Do that! My point is this is *your* path to choose and make the most of.

In my tiny orbit of work, escapades, and misadventures, it is my sincere hope that I can continue to demonstrate this ethos not only to my students and colleagues in Myanmar but to anyone out there who has taken the time to read these musings. This is for someone who might just need that extra little bit of support and cheerleading in their corner. I'm here. You've got this.

———

Discussion Questions

The author chose to remain child-free despite societal pressure and expectations. Yet despite feeling confident in her decision, she still had moments when she questioned whether something was wrong with her as a woman, since she didn't want children. As the years have passed, however, she's built a fulfilling life and career, including mentoring and "mothering" (in her own way) the students to whom she teaches EFL.

1. How did the author's relationship with her mother shape her own life vision and thoughts about having children? How have your family's expectations of you shaped the choices you've made?

2. The author ended up developing important relationships with her students that sometimes felt akin to family. What are your thoughts about chosen family versus biological family? Is one more important than the other?

6

ALL YOU NEED IS ONE

MELISSA CONNELLY

It's easy to feel like you don't count as infertile when you're a lesbian. They call it "social infertility" now, which is defined as "infertility shaped by a person's relationships and circumstances rather than a purely physiological diagnosis." But considering how it feels, social is the last adjective I would have chosen.

When I was younger, I envisioned a faceless man at the end of the aisle and a life complete with a happy marriage and 2.5 kids. I thought I'd get engaged and then get married a year later. A year after that, we would have kids. Picture-perfect. A lifelong Jehovah's Witness up to that point, I also pictured us as a family of four going to worship three times a week. My mom would be proud, and I would be happy. My plan was carefully calculated with the only variable being the groom. I'm still not sure whether that was my dream or my mother's. But no matter how hard I prayed, the older I got, the less I saw a groom at the end of the aisle.

I came out of the closet when I was twenty. This revelation effectively broke my relationship and ties to my family. But what did that mean for my dream? I still wanted that movie-magic moment. I wanted the wedding dress. I wanted to promise forever. I still wanted a family.

I remember wishing that coming out came with a guide-book. Back in 2004, gay marriage wasn't even legal. There were no same-sex couples depicted in the media, let alone same-sex families. There was just Ellen, and she had enough on her plate!

As I navigated the beginning stages of dating women in my twenties, my friends' wedding invitations started coming in the mail. By my late twenties, the wedding invitations became baby shower invites. I was overjoyed for my friends and elated to be a part of their happiness. Amidst all their joy, a small part of me still hoped that one day I would have kids of my own. But what would that look like?

My whole life, I had wanted to experience pregnancy. My desire only intensified as I bounced babies, changed diapers, and offered my babysitting services to all my friends with children. But I always thought I had more time. Doesn't everyone in their early thirties feel younger than they actually are? That's the cruel part about fertility; it decreases while you're busy making other plans.

Sure, I made certain that my conversations throughout the course of several relationships broached the subject of kids. Did they want kids? Would they want to be the one who carried the baby? These conversations were always casual, referencing some distant, more adult version of myself. Or at least that was the case until I met my wife, Kimberly.

When we met, I knew I had found the love of my life, someone who I was certain was my future. Luckily for me, when she pictured our lives together, she pictured children too. By this point, I was thirty-five, still deluding myself and holding on to the idea that time wasn't really relevant to having a baby.

Thinking about having children as a lesbian already requires a higher-than-average amount of planning. And sadly, the concept of "trying" to have a baby for a same-sex couple is a lot less fun than it is for my straight counterparts. Picture a cold procedure room with your legs in stirrups, spent with someone who did not buy you dinner first. And planning to grow a family as a same-sex couple over thirty-five is a whole new ballgame. My wife, a seasoned registered nurse, told me frankly that if we followed my timeline (with a firm refusal to feel any sort of urgency about it), we wouldn't start trying for children until I was almost forty. And that further-more, there was no guarantee I would fall pregnant on the first try. Allow me to confirm that the truth does indeed hurt!

What hurts more than the truth about your own decreasing fertility, however, is the truth about how much it costs to have a baby when your marriage is short on sperm. All I could think about was how, within socks all over Amer-ica, there was ample sperm going to waste. Yet here I was, looking at spending the down payment on a Ford Focus just to try for a baby. My wife and I started looking into how much vials of sperm cost (an average of $1,200 a vial) and calcu-lating how many we might need in our attempts to become pregnant. Keep in mind, the average couple struggling to get pregnant is told to try intrauterine insemination (IUI) at least six times before resorting to in vitro fertilization (IVF). Ka-ching! Next, we started looking into what our insurance would and wouldn't cover. In our research, we found that IVF offered patients higher success rates than IUI. However, when we started our journey, my insurance would not cover IVF until we had six failed attempts with IUI. Ka-ching, ka-ching!

After finding out that only 10 to 20 percent of people conceive on their first round of IUI, I begrudgingly agreed to make an appointment with a reproductive endocrinologist to start the process when we returned from our honeymoon. We got back from Mexico, sundrenched, in love, and optimistic. Sadly, though, nothing zaps the sex appeal out of baby-making like sitting with a masked reproductive endocrinologist who is mechanically and unenthusiastically walking you through the IUI protocol.

Our first experience left me feeling like a number instead of a person. I only met my doctor once, and we spent a total of twenty minutes together. I've had speed-dates that lasted longer. Kimberly and I were also told we had to schedule an appointment with a psychologist before we could even start the process. Even though this is standard for anyone using a third party to conceive, it still felt invasive. My mind wandered back to old college friends who were thrust into parenthood unprepared and unsure, without even the thought of mandatory therapy or requisite education. Yet I had to consult a psychologist and have them sign off.

Growing up, when you imagine starting a family, the best-case scenario involves a passionate evening that results in a positive pregnancy test. Never once did I picture that "a little help" would include mandatory psychological evaluation. I will never forget having to answer the question, "Do you or your wife have family or a good support system to help with your child?" Now, I'm a firm believer that it takes a village to raise a child. But sitting on Zoom (thanks, COVID), talking to a stranger about your homophobic family, and defending your ability to parent despite that, is a moment I will never forget.

Once we had jumped through all the requisite counseling and blood panel draws, I was told to track my period and ovulation, and then call when I ovulated and come in. My first IUI procedure was done by an RN whose bifocals, eyesight, and ability I seriously questioned. For starters, she referenced my "husband" when she was confirming my sperm sample, even though my paperwork clearly has my wife's information on it. I know; we checked.

That first two-week wait was easy. I was all hope and not a lot of expectation. It was our first try. I've always been called lucky, but even I reasoned no one is that lucky. Still, when I got my period, I cried. I cried for my wife, and I cried for myself.

As much as I hate to admit it, I felt like the magic I always believed that I possessed fell short that day.

However, after a second failed IUI attempt, luck was back on my side. My company introduced new fertility insurance coverage that would waive the six-IUI minimum and instantly approve coverage for IVF treatment. I still can't quite describe the joy and hope I felt that day. I practically skipped and leaped all over the damn house, shrieking to my wife that we could now afford IVF! I assure you there's no exaggeration in that description. Chances are, since you're reading a book that discusses infertility, you already know what a blessing that level of coverage is.

As we moved forward with IVF, we decided to change providers. Looking back at our journey, I'll be the one to loudly say that just because the hospital system is right for your insurance doesn't mean it's the right network for you. I personally like my medical staff to remember I have a wife and not a husband, but maybe that's not a dealbreaker for some people.

After extensive research, I booked my first consultation for IVF at my new provider exactly four days after my new coverage began. I met Dr. Nash on a sunny Friday afternoon. Like the other doctor, he got my pants down without the promise of a meal or shared glass of wine. But he promised me something better. He promised me that he would do everything he could to ensure my best chance at having a healthy pregnancy and a healthy baby. The difference in the treatment I got at that visit versus the previous one was like night and day. He remembered I had a wife, for starters. I became a person instead of a patient number. Yes, there were the familiar blood panels and testing, but we discussed what the results actually meant and how they would affect my fertility journey.

Most people are familiar with the fact that IVF requires you to inject yourself with a cocktail of various hormones. I'm one of those fortunate people who don't have a fear of needles or hesitation over injecting myself. What I do have is an appreciation for my sanity, which I can sadly report suffered due to the hormone shots. Knowing that you logically shouldn't be upset or sad about something but having absolutely no control over that emotion is something I always expected came with pregnancy. I did not think it would be a side effect of the meds it takes to get pregnant. I could go from mid laugh to an all-out sob, with no warning or explanation. To my wife, all I can say is thank you for loving me.

By the final day of my IVF hormone shots, I was moody and frazzled. I remember that morning vividly, as I mindlessly took a shortcut on my normal routine: get out injection needle, draw hormone, set aside, repeat, and then check all meds before injecting. The night before my egg retrieval, I had accidentally drawn the wrong hormone with the needle and gave myself a double dose of Menopur! I broke down into hysterical sobs, convinced that at the end of the whole stims process (to stimulate my ovaries), I'd fried my eggs right before the finish line. Those two hours between my frantic call to the doctor and him assuring me I was fine felt like another two-week wait.

When we found out they'd been able to retrieve fourteen eggs, I was beyond relieved. The clinic told me they would update me on how many eggs matured and then fertilized the following day. While it's common to lose a few eggs in this process, I lost twelve. Finding out I'd gone from fourteen eggs to two was heart-wrenching. Worse still, I had to hope that both eggs made it to the blastocyst stage. Was I emotionally and mentally prepared to repeat the process if they didn't make it? I barely breathed over the next six days. Your whole life, you hear the adage, "Don't put all your eggs in one basket." Well, my basket only had two little eggs to begin with.

We found out on day six that only one embryo made it. We decided to genetically test it, the results of which would take fourteen days to receive. My wife was amazing during those two weeks. We filled them with fun date nights out—including a good glass of wine—and we both tried to take our minds off it.

I received the email from my doctor's office right at the end of my workday and cried the whole way home. We had one genetically normal embryo. It took everything I could not to blurt out the good news the instant I walked in the front door of our home—especially when the good news had me positively glowing. I poured my wife and myself a drink, and I told her we were celebrating. Our motto became, "So you're saying there's a chance." I know that some people call it toxic positivity when you tell them, "All it takes is one." But when you only have one, you need to believe in that possibility. You need to hold on to that hope. It's your baby; if you don't believe in it, who else is going to?

I wish I could explain the calm I experienced after the transfer. I knew I had done everything I could to give myself the best odds there were. I just had to trust my body. I talked to my tummy. I told our baby how much they were wanted. I told them about my wife and myself, and how the house we'd bought that summer would be the home they'd grow up in. I told them how very much they were loved. It might sound silly to you, but I've always believed in manifesting and that I possess a little bit of magic. It's a childlike belief that I hope I never lose and that I can share with our children someday.

After the transfer, we had to wait ten days to find out if I was pregnant, which meant we would get the news the day after Thanksgiving. As we went about shopping and preparing our menu for the holiday dinner, I kept thinking, *I could be pregnant right now.* I tried convincing my wife to let me test Thanksgiving morning. By my reasoning, we could be *extra* thankful that year! My wife, a brilliant nurse, reminded me that blood tests are more reliable and an at-home test might give us a false negative. I could possibly ruin my own Thanksgiving for nothing.

I made it six days before cornering my wife as she got ready to leave for a work trip. "I'll crack like an egg and test the instant you leave the house," I said. "So you can either find out *with* me or *after* me. The choice is yours."

Kim looked at me one last time and reiterated, "You realize it might say you're not pregnant yet, even if you are?" I nodded and told her I understood but I still wanted to take the test. We stood there at 4:30 a.m., waiting for the timer to go off. We got our two pink lines on November 22, 2021.

Our one little embryo had finally given us a successful pregnancy, and the message was loud and clear: All we'd needed was one.

Discussion Questions

The author writes about the discomfort and microaggressions she experienced while trying to start a family as part of a lesbian couple—from the use of the term "social infertility" to medical professionals automatically referencing her husband instead of wife. She also talks about the roller coaster of the process, and how they ended up with only one viable embryo —but still maintained a sense of optimism and never gave up hope.

1. Have you ever experienced discrimination with a medical provider or, like the author, felt more like a number than a person? How did you handle this? Did you feel empowered to take any action? Why or why not?
2. The author says that throughout the process, her motto was, "So you're saying there's a chance." Do you tend to have a more optimistic or pessimistic outlook? How do you think this impacts your life?

7

FROM GRACE TO GRACE

ERIN KOELLIKER

Hope was embedded within my bones from before I was born. I was raised in a religious home in a religious community, and ancestors in my family lines were some of the pioneers who trekked barefoot across the frozen rivers of the Midwestern United States in long wagon trains. Tales of their unimaginable sacrifice and strength filled my childhood. At church, at home around the dinner table, and in school, I heard stories about the pioneers, saw their stern expressions in faded black-and-white photographs, and marveled at what possibly could have moved them forward when I probably would have stopped.

My ancestors, as admirable and worthy as they were, were not wholly unique. Human history is crowded with brave immigrants who left what they knew with the hope of finding something better. But it's taken me until adulthood—and specifically parenthood—to understand the impact that this personal tradition of hope has had on me.

I have never done anything as heroic as fleeing persecution or as hopeful as moving to a new country in search of a new life. But I did keep trying when I was terrified and wanted to stop. And I did move forward even when I knew my life would be easier if I didn't risk so much of myself in the process. The instinct to try comes from the innate mindset that was nurtured within me since birth, and it's the same instinct that taught me to expect to find a source of light in the dark.

Henry

I don't know of a more hopeful time in my life than when I was pregnant for the first time. My husband, Rob, and I had been married for four years when I became pregnant with our first child in the summer of 2009. At the time, our intent was to create something special—so that with this child, and hopefully more down the road, we would be building the home and family life of our dreams.

My pregnancy was unremarkable, with only minor concerns along the way. All the usual symptoms like nausea, heartburn, and fatigue were present, and I took comfort in watching my swollen belly grow and feeling occasional kicks.

Looking back, much of what made that first pregnancy special was the relationship I had with my obstetrician. I had been a patient of hers for a couple of years before I was pregnant, but I felt like we truly bonded as my pregnancy progressed. She essentially is the ob-gyn of your dreams: personable and warm, professional and smart, and always quick to laugh or give you a hug. I knew that my health, and most importantly, my baby's health, were in good hands with her.

And as the weeks ticked forward, I couldn't wait to meet our baby boy, whom we had decided to name Henry Robert. When I envisioned him, it was always with blonde, curly hair—a son who would surely be as intelligent and noble as his name.

I labored in the hospital for eight hours with Henry, and after I became fully dilated, my doctor appeared in my room and told me that it was time to break my water. When the nurses broke the sac, they noticed that there was meconium in it—the black, tar-like substance babies produce after they're born, but normally not when they're in utero. I was told that this was nothing to worry about, because Henry's and my heart scans had been completely normal. From almost the minute I checked in to labor and delivery, a disc-like sensor was placed on my belly to track Henry's heart rate, and it was assuredly predictable and steady.

There was no way of knowing how crucial and precious the next hour would be. Rob and I had packed a camcorder in my hospital bag, but we didn't bring it out. Caught up in the euphoria and perfection of the moment, we assumed we would have time to film Henry later. If he had been born now when everyone has a smartphone, we could have at least caught most or some of my labor, even if only through pictures. As it was, I pushed for forty-five minutes, and through the searing pain of unmedicated childbirth, I visualized my chubby, blonde-headed baby with curly hair without feeling the need to film anything.

Part of me wishes that we had documented the event that would change my life. There is Erin before Henry's birth, and there is Erin after Henry's birth. The trauma of his birth took away the innocence and ease that had dictated my life up to that point, and the shock of witnessing what came next would fundamentally change my worldview. I wish I had documentation to review what was said or done during those moments when my life changed without my permission.

But I do have memories.

Initially, Henry's head came out without any problem. But as I kept pushing, my doctor saw that the umbilical cord was wrapped around his neck. She tried loosening the cord with her fingers, but eventually she pulled Henry's broad shoulders out of me in the middle of a fierce contraction in order to get the cord free. And it was then that I learned I was right. Henry did have blonde, curly hair. He was six-and-a-half pounds and absolute perfection. Up until that point, the room had been a hive of activity and noise, with grunting and yelping from me along with encouragement and cheers from Rob, my mom, and my doctor in between pushes.

But then, there was silence.

My doctor hurriedly told Rob to cut the cord and just as quickly passed Henry off to a team of specialists who had been called in from the newborn intensive care unit (NICU). Rob and I gaped stupidly as two nurses performed CPR on our baby, who was not even five minutes old. A baby I hadn't even seen yet. In the corner of my delivery room, the NICU team worked on Henry in an open incubator and stabilized his breathing long enough for Rob to see him clearly for the first time. And while Rob's back was to me, I repeatedly asked my doctor if Henry was going to be alright.

She didn't know. No one knew the extent of the damage that those first breathless moments could wreak on his body or how they would impact the next four days. What we did know was that Henry needed CPR again, and he needed immediate help in the NICU.

On that first day—the day of Henry's birth—Rob and I were hopeful. We were anxious and in shock, but we believed that Henry would ultimately be fine. No one we knew had experienced childbirth like this, but people reassured us that they had heard of a cousin or family friend or someone else who had the cord around their neck during birth, and they were now an adult or a grandmother or a professional drummer. Whatever they were, they were fine and had led full and happy lives. That Henry's course could be different never occurred to us. Even after the neonatologist talked with us and gently explained that Henry was in bad shape, we clung to the anecdotal comments of other survivors and believed in them like guarantees.

But Henry's condition worsened. Since he was hooked up to a ventilator, we couldn't hold him or cuddle like we had expected to do. We could only sit by his bedside and stare at him.

At first, we would comment on how healthy he looked and how he would surely only be in the NICU for a day or two, a week at most, and then we would take him home. But as the beeps and blares of his machines became louder and more urgent, we looked for answers. No doctor, nurse, or specialist had a definitive reason as to why Henry was in such critical condition. In the absence of a diagnosis, Rob and I clung to our family for support, and we prayed and pleaded for Henry's health.

In the middle of the third night, Henry started to have seizures. He was sedated and on pain medication to keep him comfortable, and he hadn't opened his eyes since the day of his birth.

By day four, Rob and I were given results from an MRI that found that our beautiful baby had extensive bleeding on his brain. The bleeding was putting so much pressure on his skull that it was causing seizures and systematically shutting down his body. He was in danger of going into cardiac arrest, and we needed to let the staff know what our wishes were if Henry had to be resuscitated again.

The NICU staff tried to explain Henry's condition to us with sensitivity and compassion, but I spent much of that afternoon sobbing. Up until the moment that we were told of his brain bleed, I believed that he may have a disability or need more medical interventions throughout his life, but I also assumed he would still live. It wasn't until we talked with a family friend who was also a neonatologist in the NICU that Rob and I fully understood what Henry was up against, and together we came to the same conclusion: It was time for Henry to breathe on his own. We wanted it to be his decision, not ours, as to how long he would live and how long he would fight for air. We also knew it wouldn't be for long.

Life had been so unfair to him. When I looked at his

perfect face that night, I thought about how confused he must have felt to not be held and swaddled close to his parents like all babies wanted. I thought about how unnatural his life had been. The NICU stimulated each of my senses, and all in traumatic ways. Henry lived in a noisy, open hospital unit—away from our family and friends—and it was jarring to be in that environment. I realized that Henry wouldn't sleep in his crib that Rob had set up for him after Christmas or sit in the car seat that we had installed in our sedan. I felt like Henry had been robbed and I had been punched in the stomach by an iron glove studded with metal spikes. But what came next truly was the hardest part.

One of the foundational principles of my religion is that there is life after death. I knew this to be true when Henry died, and I felt certain that, even as I kissed him goodbye for the last time, I would see him again. But I also knew I was only twenty-five years old and still had many years ahead of me before I could be reunited with my baby. The weight of this realization seemed insurmountable and threatened to drown me on my darkest days.

Over those first weeks, I went through stages where I didn't want to go to bed, because I cried to strangers in my dreams. Then I went through a phase where all I wanted to do was sleep, because at least in my sleep, I didn't have to think. And for four solid months after Henry's death, I felt like my body and my mind took turns sleeping while I was awake. I was a zombie who was constantly crying or on the brink of crying, and each day felt interminably long. And though I was rarely by myself, I had never felt so lonely and misunderstood.

Painting my nails helped. So did walking our little dog that we adopted shortly after Henry died. I had never been confronted with such intense emotions, and it helped when my loved ones nudged me in a helpful direction. They took me out to lunch, brought Rob and me dinner, took us to the movies, and went on long walks with me. Sunday drives, trips out of town, meals at one or two in the morning with Rob, and many screaming sessions in the car also helped. And when I got a new job in a fast-paced environment and my coworkers and bosses patiently listened to me and guided me out of my stupor, that revived my brain and helped me regain my energy.

Trying Again

I wish there were a way to sidestep grief or that I could tell you a secret to make the pain go away. But if there is one, I didn't find it. One year out from Henry's death, I was in an ugly and unfamiliar place. I felt nothing like the fabled pioneers, some of whom had buried their children along the trail, not knowing if they would ever be able to revisit their gravesides. But all the while, they stoically did their duty and retained their faith.

I started to feel like I was not being "graceful" in my grief. I was stuck in a position of wanting to be an example of my personal faith—which was still intact—while also being realistic with my experience of unexpected loss. When I measured myself against other people in the news, on social media, and in my personal life, I felt like I was failing. The image of a stalwart, faithful mother who went about life carrying loss and not letting it get her down was an expectation that wasn't within my reach. I felt guilty about shutting people out and holding onto my anger longer than what was viewed as "normal." I felt I was not living up to the lofty standards of my faithful ancestors, who took loss after loss and somehow kept going in dignity.

The truth was that I was familiar with so many heroic stories of men and women overcoming tragedy but never stopped to think how that must have actually felt for them. I had skipped over the ugly parts—the raw, emotional ones, where even men and women from the beginning of time had mourned their children and felt all the feelings associated with living, dying, and burying their loved ones.

Around this time, I began to go down a train of thought that wasn't particularly helpful. I would think, *Hey, I'm a good person. If there is a purpose in the hard parts of my life, what was the big lesson in losing my baby? Couldn't I have gone through something else that was less devastating?* I planted this thought deep within me, placing it with bitterness and watering it with anger. Then I nourished it with self-pity until it blossomed into a part of me that I didn't recognize.

None of my emotions or feelings were bad or wrong. I knew that then, and I know that now. They were all natural and even expected after having my baby die.

They were also so large I couldn't contain them. As I tried to process my grief, I turned inward and attempted to repair the damage by myself. But the more I focused on myself, the more frustrated I would get. The more righteous and indignant anger I funneled into my situation, the more cheated and hostile I felt. I wasn't supposed to be painting my nails every other day; I was supposed to be changing diapers. I didn't want to go on a walk by myself; all I wanted was to walk my baby. And if I couldn't walk him, then I wanted to care for another one.

It took me a little over a year to become pregnant again, but it felt much longer than that. I'd cry each month when my period started, and I wanted to be pregnant again so desperately that I would convince myself, even despite evidence to the contrary, that my aches or cramps were symptoms of early pregnancy. At around this time, I began to compulsively buy pregnancy and ovulation tests from a local dollar store. I would take test after test after test in a futile attempt to know the exact moment I would or could get pregnant.

Rob and I bought our first house in 2011, and as we did some DIY renovations, we began to feel hopeful. We had a home—a place for our own memories and family to continue growing.

We moved into our new house right as I learned I was pregnant. Our instincts were to keep the pregnancy quiet and get further along, but a dauntless group of family and friends had rallied behind us since Henry, and we wanted to share our joy with them and have something to celebrate.

Forty weeks felt like a long wait for us to meet our next child. We had been assured by my doctors and Henry's that his death was a freak accident and unlikely to happen again, but we were anxious. Since we didn't know what had been the exact cause of Henry's death, I fretted over what to eat and what to avoid. I didn't know if his death had something to do with a choice I'd made while pregnant, but I wanted to be sure that I made no mistakes this time. I wanted to make it full-term—to hold that baby and look it in the eye, knowing I did everything I could to help it get here safely.

Toward the end of September, I was eleven weeks pregnant, and Rob was on a business trip in Taiwan. One morning while at work, I went to the bathroom and noticed a large spot of clotted, brown blood in my underwear. I was able to get an ultrasound for that same day, and I tried to be brave. If I had thoughts about the worst happening, I would forcefully push them out of my head and think of a happy scenario. This, I thought, was surely going to be OK. It was a scare and nothing more.

But when I looked at the screen and saw the curling shape of my little fetus, my fears were confirmed. The baby didn't have a heartbeat. Sobbing, I woke Rob in Taiwan, and we began to mourn the death of another dream. I spent the rest of that week before my surgery lying on my couch, alternating between crying and sleeping.

Rob made it home for my surgery, and as I woke up from general anesthesia in the recovery room, a kind nurse checked my vitals and asked me questions to help me regain consciousness. I answered her with as much lucidity as I could muster. I don't recall most of them, but I do remember her asking me if this was my first pregnancy. In my fog, fresh from a surgery to remove a miscarried baby, I told her no. She looked stricken with sadness when I told her about Henry, and I remember that she touched my forehead and smoothed my hair. With compassion, she looked at me and said, "Oh, honey. Go back to sleep."

A month later, we learned that the autopsy results had come back, and we had a definitive answer as to why my body miscarried. The baby had Trisomy 21, or Down syndrome. From then on, my pregnancies were going to be considered high risk.

Eddie

We didn't tell people about our baby having Down syndrome. After Henry, we'd made ourselves vulnerable, confiding to strangers or new acquaintances and sharing the most tender moments of our lives. It was almost like there had been a window over my heart, leaving it constantly on display—my pain visible and readily seen by others. I didn't want this to be construed as a character flaw, but I also couldn't get over it yet. If others knew about our baby having Down syndrome, people would worry that much more about me if I got pregnant again. Family members might ask more pointed questions or might even doubt my choices about having more children, and I was too fragile for that type of scrutiny.

In truth, this scrutiny was imagined. Our loved ones were too concerned with our well-being to be judgmental, but I didn't like the feeling of being so different from my family. My siblings and in-laws had certainly tackled their own challenges and heartaches but not like we had. Although I had plenty of things in common with the people I was closest to, I had been through one too many dramatic events, which made it difficult for them to fully identify with me or my pain.

Remember that plant that I had nourished earlier? The bitter one that questioned why I needed to take such a beating in my life to learn anything? It became a full-grown sycamore tree by Thanksgiving 2011.

One month later, I was pregnant again, and this time I was full-on nervous. My compulsions for finding control were in high gear, and I took seven pregnancy tests to confirm my pregnancy. Until I got to twelve weeks gestation, I also used my reliable dollar store pregnancy tests each week to ease my mind that I was still pregnant. Things had gone so wrong with the others, surely this was our chance. Out of the many emotions that I was confronted with, I chose to cling to hope to help me get through the anxieties that found me each day.

My son Eddie was born at twenty-eight weeks weighing two-and-a-half pounds. He was in the NICU for sixty-one days, the same place where Henry had lived and died. When we finally took Eddie home, he was five pounds, and we were terrified. We had never had a baby in our home before, let alone one who needed supplemental oxygen and had a compromised immune system.

We quarantined with Eddie in 2012 and into 2013 before it became a legitimate thing with COVID. He was at high risk of RSV, which would have wreaked havoc on his tiny body. During the respiratory season (October through April), we stayed away from our family and friends and kept Eddie inside. His only times out were in the car and at his doctors' appointments.

Over time, he gained weight and grew. Holding him, loving him, and watching him grow healed a lot of what was broken.

When Eddie was a year and a half old, a friend invited me to do a service project with her. She had been on hospitalized bed rest with her first child, and her twins had spent time in the NICU over Christmas. She thought it would be nice to put little care packages together for moms who had NICU babies and were on hospitalized bed rest for the holidays, so they wouldn't feel lonely. Our project, now called Kits of Love, is a 501(c)3 nonprofit, and since 2013, we've only missed one Christmas of showering moms and dads with love. We get local and corporate businesses to donate items to our kits and raise money grassroots-style from our family and friends. Two years ago, we also received a grant that enabled us to buy fifty car seats for single moms or low-income families, most of them immigrants.

While each kit is unique, they typically contain cozy socks, lip balm, dry shampoo, lotion, something to read, and of course, chocolate. We average about 150 to 200 kits per year and deliver them in person to parents at five hospitals. The parents who we see are emotional and scared out of their minds but also so proud of their amazing preemies.

Seeing them, hearing their stories, and learning about their children is the best part. We give kits, but more than that, we give hope. We tell them that we know how they feel and that we've been where they've been, and we've survived. We cheer them on, give them a hug, and invite them to stay in contact with us. Aside from my work as a mother, this is the job I am the most proud of in my life.

Thomas

By the time I was pregnant with my third son, Tom, I no longer trusted my own body. I had a cerclage placed when I was nineteen weeks pregnant—a procedure designed to keep the cervix closed and prevent early labor—and I received progesterone shots each week. I saw my high-risk doctor very regularly and also had frequent ultrasounds. Even with all of that attention and excellent care, I was horrified that I might have another early baby, and I didn't know how I would be able to balance keeping Eddie healthy at home and seeing my tiny baby in the hospital. The cerclage, the worry, the trauma —all of it (or maybe none of it) combined into constant contractions. Each time the contractions worsened and wouldn't go away, I had to go to the ER to get checked and make sure I wasn't in labor—which was seven times.

We planned for a lot of different scenarios for Tommy's birth in case he needed to go to the NICU. He was going to be born at thirty-six weeks, and my doctor told me to mentally prepare myself for him needing to go to the NICU.

But Tom ended up being my only baby who didn't need to go to the NICU. His birth was incredibly healing for me, and I loved having two healthy boys in my home.

Margaret

My pregnancy with my daughter Maggie was a happy surprise. Then at six weeks, I hemorrhaged when I was cleaning our house and bled through my underwear, through my pants, and down my legs. I felt like I was going to lose another baby, but after an ultrasound, she appeared to be fine. For weeks, I was on high alert for signs of another loss. Thankfully they didn't come, and the baby continued to develop.

At seventeen weeks, I began to contract again and had another cerclage placed. This helped keep the baby in, but I contended with regular contractions again and was put on bed rest.

Before I was on bed rest, I always thought it sounded glamorous and nice. But it is neither of those things, particularly when you have two other children that you'd like to take care of. I would lay in my bed and worry and second-guess myself. Again, I didn't trust my body. Again, I went to the ER (five times this time around) to make sure I wasn't in labor. Each time I went, my knees would knock together, and my

teeth would chatter in fear of delivering another early baby—
or worse, losing another one.

This pregnancy was physically and mentally the hardest.
Although our little girl was developing well, I was anxious and
had to talk myself down from hysterics, because I was
convinced that something was going to happen to her or go
wrong. I lived in chronic fear, and a week before she was born,
I felt so horrified she was going to die that I ended up
messaging the wonderful doctor who delivered Henry.

Somehow, even though she was in a remote part of
Canada, she got my message and wrote me back. I don't know
why I felt compelled to reach out to her, but I knew she would
help me feel peace. She knew my heart. She knew my anxieties and the stress I was battling. She was also kind, and I
trusted she could calm me down. She did. And she happens to
be Dr. Angela Chaudhari, another contributor to this book. I
will love her forever.

Being pregnant with my children and being their mother
through their first fragile days and weeks has truly tested my
ability to remain hopeful. I want to make it clear that the
experiences that I've shared are coming from the comfortable
place of looking backward. From my current vantage point, it
has been over a decade since my first pregnancy and five years
since my last. My babies can in no way be categorized as
babies anymore, so the intensely protective feeling of caring
for a baby in my womb or a newborn in my arms isn't as fresh
as it once was.

Time has healed much of what was broken within me,
and even though everything terrible hasn't magically been
made better, the past eleven years have been a buffer from the
anguish that came after loss. My losses and heartaches were
and are significant, but they're no longer recent, and that
makes a difference.

But perspective is different than perfection. By sharing
these memories with you now, I am reopening a fragile vein

that I've been trying to stop from bleeding out too frequently. These memories not only make me feel vulnerable when I write about them, but they also transport me back into situations that are profoundly sad. Still, as stressful as they are to relive, these memories have also become sacred. Certain parts of my life that once felt insurmountable have become doable and even beautiful over time, encouraging me to review each memory with hopeful eyes. My greatest hope is that by telling this story, besides making my family proud, I will help you or someone you love to find light in the dark.

Discussion Questions

The author experienced child loss and multiple traumatic births, yet she has the family she always dreamt of and the gift of time when it comes to healing. Along the way, she transformed some of her grief into hope by founding an organization that delivers gifts to families spending their holidays in the NICU.

1. The author writes about feeling like she's not grieving in the right way, that her grief is too visible, and that she's letting down her ancestors— who, in her mind, faced much greater hardships. What do you think about this? Is there a right way to grieve?

2. The author mentions the healing power of time. Can you think of a hardship in your life about which you now have a different perspective after some time has passed? How has your perspective on it changed?

8

AN INTERNATIONAL DANCE

TRAFFORD JUDD

It was seven o'clock on an unusually clear Seattle morning. My husband, Mike, and I drove in silence over the long, straight bridge that links Seattle with Bellevue. From the passenger seat, I stared out at the brilliant blue of Lake Washington. Then, in the rearview mirror of our rented Ford Explorer, I caught a glimpse of the empty baby carrier in the backseat. It had been there for weeks as we explored this unfamiliar city, trying to fill the days and distract ourselves from a perpetual state of anxiety, boredom, anticipation, and hope.

Mike and I met in 2004 on our first day of university class in Melbourne, Australia. When I arrived, I noticed a tall, good-looking guy in a purple T-shirt across the room. After the lecture, the purple-clad man asked me if I felt like sharing a bowl of noodle soup at the local Malaysian restaurant. From that day on, Mike and I were inseparable, first as friends and then as more.

Ten years later, we had completed our studies, traveled the world, and built a rich and fulfilling life together. We owned a stylish townhome, drove a cute Peugeot sports car, walked a fluffy Lhasa apso twice a day while sipping coffee, and had established careers that gave us the disposable income to travel, eat, and do whatever we wanted. At times, I felt guilty for the privileged life we had attained, which was so far beyond what I even thought possible for myself while growing up in rural New South Wales. Life was easy. Life was good.

Of course, nothing stays peaceful for long. Right around that ten-year mark, Mike's dad, who had been diagnosed with multiple sclerosis at thirty but had remained healthy for decades, was admitted to the hospital with pneumonia. After a few weeks, it became clear he was nearing the end of his life. We said our goodbyes and made funeral plans. That same weekend, my father suffered a near-fatal heart attack while on a camping trip and was rushed to hospital for emergency bypass surgery.

It sounds cliché, but after the trauma of losing one parent and then nearly losing another, Mike and I started to reflect on the meaning of our own existences. Both of our fathers had built fulfilling lives, pierced by hardship but enriched by the eternal anchor of family and a wide group of friends. And although we were fortunate to have maintained close and supportive relationships with our families—by no means a given for gay couples like us—we started wondering if attending our nieces' and nephews' birthday parties was enough. When we became our fathers' ages, would we look back with a longing for the anchor of our own family?

So, one night over seared scallops and Sancerre, we broached the topic we'd been tiptoeing around for weeks. By the end of the evening, we'd proposed a toast to *family*, and on the drive home, Mike googled how to fit a baby seat in the back of a two-door car. Like so much of what was to come, the answer was complicated.

Research skills are perhaps the most important prerequisite for same-sex couples thinking about creating a family. Not knowing where to begin, we found ourselves on a cold winter morning at our local town hall, at what was essentially a job fair—if the only job on offer was that of becoming a parent.

Dozens of mostly male couples gathered to explore their options and hear the stories of those who had gone before them. The booths were made up of a strange mix of religious-based foster care agencies (who, while courting our services as foster parents, were also part of the infrastructure actively lobbying against our right to marry), overseas surrogacy agencies from India and the United States, and auxiliary services such as day care providers, private schools, baby supply stores, and government services.

Rather than coming away inspired, I left feeling overwhelmed—both at the number of options and the work it would require to make any of them a reality. On one hand, it was nice to hear from couples who were far along on their parenting journey, but on the other, it was depressing to see the complexity involved in achieving what for many people is literally achieved by accident. It was clear that if we were to have any chance of making our dream a reality, we'd need organization, resilience, and a lot of time.

Mike's family has long been involved with the foster care sector. His mother, Sue, has fostered over fifty children and was awarded a Medal of the Order of Australia for her service to the community through foster care. She told us how fostering had enriched her life in unimaginable ways, but also noted how the grief of having to give children back to their parents, often into less-than-ideal circumstances, would have been too much to bear had she not had her own "forever family." As we reflected on our own motivations for starting a family in the first place—to add a new long-term dimension to our lives—fostering as our sole experience of parenthood didn't seem like the right fit.

We explored adoption next but quickly felt defeated. At the time, Australia didn't permit adoption by same-sex parents (a policy that was overturned in 2018). What initially seemed like an obvious approach was quickly ruled out. Our options were narrowing.

There were two pathways to parenthood left for us: coparenting and surrogacy. However, our desire for a small, intimate nuclear family wasn't compatible with the expansiveness of coparenting. So with all other options crossed off the list, we set our sights on the unknown world of surrogacy.

At the time, in our state of Victoria and throughout Australia, surrogacy laws were Byzantine and rapidly changing. We read forums, made connections with others who'd been through it, and spoke with an attorney who'd been successful at navigating the complex legal landscape to secure parenting rights for families formed via surrogacy. A few pages of notes turned into a full notebook, which spawned a folder and eventually a compendium of definitions, process maps, resources, and medical documentation, as well as referrals to IVF clinics, surrogacy and egg donor agencies, lawyers, insurers, government agencies, literature, and more.

Once you open the Pandora's Box of surrogacy, it's impossible to avoid taking a mental audit of all the childbearing females in your life. We started with family: I come from a family of four brothers, and while I had several close female friends, none were at the life stage where I would be comfortable even broaching the subject with them. Mike has four sisters, but they all had families of their own, were approaching forty, and had busy home and work lives. We really couldn't think of a single person we knew who met all the criteria, let alone someone with whom we would feel comfortable embarking on this journey. So we decided to look into what, at the time, felt like a last resort: "commercial" surrogacy.

Words matter, and the use of that term felt dirty, as if we were renting a womb, not intentionally creating a human life in partnership within an informed and intimate team committed to making this happen. And in 2012 when we first started this journey, commercial surrogacy laws were changing rapidly around the world, and it wasn't legal in Australia. For this reason, most of the couples we knew who'd pursued surrogacy had done so in India, which was easier to travel to than the US. Before we knew it, we were on a plane to New Delhi.

After a short, perilous drive in the town car the agency had sent for us, dodging potholes, rickshaws, street vendors, and city buses, we arrived at the agency headquarters. Our host immediately poured a steaming hot cup of sweet chai tea, the unparalleled smell of fresh cardamom permeating the room and permanently imprinting on my brain. To this day, I smell cardamom and am immediately transported to that moment, to that room, engulfed by uncertainty and expectation.

The agency seemed like a well-run operation. The facilities were sparkling clean, and the staff were friendly. The owner talked us through the process at length, answered our questions, and made us feel like this was something we could actually do. We briefly met some surrogates who were living on premises, which was standard practice during their final trimester. We were unable to speak with them due to language barriers, and the wealth disparity between us and them couldn't be ignored. This raised some ethical concerns for us —that perhaps these women felt forced to do this for the money—but we were assured otherwise by the agency. We had come this far, and with our toes already in the water, it seemed like the only choice was to dive in.

Until this point, we had decided not to tell friends and family about our journey. We're both fairly private people, and there's also a stigma around surrogacy in Australia. With all our emotional energy being channeled in that direction, we didn't have any reserves to explain to people why we were doing what we were doing, or to deal with the inevitable blow-back. In retrospect, I think we also had a bit of shame about proceeding with surrogacy in a developing country. While I didn't recognize it at the time, there are highly complex racial, gender, religious, economic, and geopolitical dynamics at play when navigating such a situation—dynamics I wish I'd been better equipped to grasp then, and even still today.

Our next step was to find a suitable egg donor who could help transform Mike's frozen sperm in New Delhi into a viable embryo. Shopping for an egg donor, to me, felt like shopping for a car. There are tons of nice cars out there, all with similar specs, and at the end of the day, they're all likely to get you where you need to go. But eventually we selected a woman from the UK named Katie. She seemed strong, independent, and well educated, and she had similar physical characteristics to us both. After wiring a not-insubstantial amount of money to the agency, Katie started her hormone therapy and was booked to travel to India six weeks later to time with the surrogate's ovarian cycle. We would never speak with Katie, but if this was successful, she would be the biological mother of our child.

Katie was due to fly from the UK to India a few days before the egg transfer. We woke up that morning to a torrent of emails from the egg donor agency, interspersed with angry replies from the surrogacy agency. According to the egg agency, Katie had failed to board her flight due to a sudden illness. No further details were available. The surrogacy agency was furious; they had, after all, a surrogate who had been preparing to have an embryo transferred in the coming days.

Things started to unravel, and we felt a roller coaster of emotions. So many questions raced through my mind, questions which would not—could not—be answered. Was Katie's illness related to the medications she had been taking to stimulate her egg production? Were we to blame for this? Then the questions took a dark turn. Was it all a scam? Had we been taken advantage of? To this day, I struggle to remember some of the details, having blocked them out in order to protect myself from the hurt, confusion, guilt, embarrassment, anger, and vulnerability that were swirling through every part of my body.

Neither Mike nor I will ever truly know what happened, but the opacity of information and lack of control left us feeling like the trust required to move forward with our current surrogacy plan had been irrevocably broken. Sleep-deprived, depleted of emotional energy, and tens of thousands of dollars in debt, we decided to walk away from the whole operation, defeated.

Several weeks passed, and we finally mustered the energy to plot our next move. There was only one other place in the world with a robust surrogacy infrastructure, and that was the United States. Up until now, the US had seemed like a fortress: a mighty entity that couldn't possibly be penetrated due to a lack of time, money, and the tyranny of distance. Besides the cost, starting our entire journey from the very beginning was almost too much to bear given the paperwork, emotional burden, and perpetual pause we had placed on so many other aspects of our lives. At the same time, this suddenly seemed like an investment—an insurance policy to never again feel the emotional anguish we had experienced to date.

Our first conversation with the agency in Los Angeles was both refreshing and a huge relief. We quickly learned that the US had a robust legal framework for commercial surrogacy arrangements, and we felt like we had a team of experts who were there to partner with us on making our dream of parent-hood a reality. Importantly, we revisited the ethical concerns we had felt throughout our journey in India. The legal protec-tion and robust psychological counseling processes in place for egg donors, the surrogate and her spouse, and us as intended parents set our minds at ease.

The agency sent us a list of surrogate profiles alongside a brief bio introducing each one and her family. One couple immediately stood out for us, both because of the wit in their introductory letter and the explicit commitment to LGBT equality stated within. Originally from Ohio, Mandy and her husband, Chris, had recently moved to Seattle, Washington, which was one of sixteen states that had an optimal legal framework to allow out-of-country, same-sex intended parents to be on the child's birth certificate from the start. The agency shared our bio with Chris and Mandy, who were equally interested in meeting. We set up a match meeting and booked flights to Los Angeles for a few weeks' time.

On our first day in LA, Mike and I parked our rental car outside a gleaming office on Wilshire Boulevard; the street's nickname, Miracle Mile, felt like an omen of things to come. We entered the lobby and could see through the frosted glass a silhouette of the strangers we were about to meet. Our account manager greeted us, then walked us in to meet Mandy and Chris. The pleasantries quickly evolved into an hour of intense, facilitated conversation covering everything from embryo reduction, Down's syndrome, termination, and more.

After a while, we were encouraged to go outside and spend some time together. We strolled the La Brea Tar Pits, drank Sam Adams lager, and ate nachos amidst the idyllic glow of a Los Angeles evening. Within a few hours, the most contrived, unnatural situation I'd ever faced evolved into one of the most natural friendships I've experienced in my life. We had a blast and dropped them back to their hotel, feeling certain that we had met our perfect match. The next morning, we eagerly confirmed our intention with the agency, and Mandy did the same. Miracle Mile had delivered exactly what it promised.

At the match meeting with Mandy, we had shared with her our decision to largely keep our surrogacy journey a secret. After all, most straight couples don't tell their loved ones until the end of the first trimester; why should we share when we hadn't even attempted to create an embryo yet? Mandy, never one to hold back an opinion, said that if it were her life, she would tell her close friends and family about every step of this journey. Speaking positive things into being, she said, had always worked for her and Chris; maybe it would work for us too. Mike and I aren't superstitious, but I've always believed that having a cold bottle of champagne in the fridge helps good things happen, so her theory didn't seem completely off base. We decided we would start sharing our journey more broadly.

Our first opportunity to put the sharing into action was at a celebration for my cousin Bec's twenty-eighth birthday. At the pub, we told Bec and her family about the true purpose of our trip to Los Angeles—and that we had found a surrogate but hadn't yet chosen an egg donor. The next morning, I received a text message from Bec. It simply read: "What about me?"

Although we had long ago completed an audit of potential surrogates, Mike and I hadn't, until that moment, considered anyone we knew as a potential egg donor. We always figured the genetic connection would be best handled at a distance. But the more I considered it, the more it made sense. Bec and I had formed a close friendship as young adults and had a lot of traits in common. Bec said she didn't feel particularly maternal, and I had no fears that she would want to be overly involved in our child's life. And, like with Mandy, the appeal of our child being able to maintain a relationship with her genetic mother seemed like a wonderful gift that, until now, we didn't even think was available to us.

Mike and I reached out to the surrogacy agency to ask what would be involved in using a known egg donor, and we immediately commenced the process. Bec would need to travel to the IVF clinic in Pasadena for the egg retrieval and subsequent transfer. Timing was important, and things were moving quickly. I was afraid Bec would feel overwhelmed, mostly because *I* was feeling overwhelmed. There were only about twelve weeks from the moment that original text message came through to the beginning of the drug cycle, and in that time, Mandy took taking hormones to improve the chances that the embryo would turn into a viable pregnancy. The timeline was complicated and reminded me of trying to step into a moving jump rope at just the right time. On the optimal day of Mandy's cycle, Bec would need to be in California—an eighteen-hour flight away—for egg retrieval, which would then be matched with Mike's thawed sperm and implanted into Mandy's uterus.

It was a complex international dance with so many moving parts that it seemed all but impossible everything would come together. But, in August 2013, Bec flew to Pasadena to meet Mandy. Mike and I stayed in Australia to save costs, but we knew our future was in good hands with these two powerful women.

The night before the embryo transfer, Bec sent an email, which I received at the beginning of my workday in Australia:

I really do hope that you receive the happiest, healthiest little bubs out of this whole process, and that all the disappointments and trial and error along the way will all seem worth it in the end. I think I can speak for both Mandy and myself when I say that we are honored and delighted to be a part of your very unique and special baby-making team. We both have unfaltering faith that the little ones will be loved, cherished, and spoilt rotten.

I spent the rest of the day crying in my office cubicle in Melbourne, thinking about these two amazing women on the other side of the Pacific Ocean and what they were doing to make our family dream a reality.

The egg retrieval was a success, and a few days later, we video-conferenced into the transfer procedure where two five-day-old embryos were inserted into Mandy's uterus. In the following days, we awoke to a daily "pee stick" update from Mandy. Eager to know her status, she sent an email each day with pictures of what turned out to be twenty-eight home pregnancy tests. Finally the time came for the two-week appointment where we would officially determine whether Mandy was pregnant.

We were asked to call the nurse immediately after Mandy's appointment, which happened to be at 3:30 a.m. our time. Bleary-eyed, we emailed the nurse, "We're awake—ready to speak when you are!" and within a minute, the phone rang from a US number. This was the call.

The nurse walked us through the numbers, letting us know that Mandy's hormone levels were much higher than what they had even hoped for. Then the words we were waiting for: "Mandy is very, very pregnant."

Going back to sleep was impossible. We walked the dog while sipping the first of many cups of coffee, waiting for the world to wake up. After a call to both grandmas, texts to siblings and a few close friends, and a flurry of excited messages with Mandy and Bec, we tried to get on with our days, unable to wipe the grins off our faces.

The next few months progressed without incident. In December, we traveled to Seattle to get to know Mandy and her family better, as well as to be present for the all-important twenty-week scan. It coincided with the Christmas holidays, and we took the opportunity to celebrate with Mandy's family. We enjoyed experiencing some of their American food traditions: blueberry salad, mac and cheese, buffalo wild wings. In return, they politely tolerated the kale salad we presented as a side dish. The scan went without a hitch, the incredible 3D images the first indication that this all was actually happening.

At the same time that our new family was beginning to form, the gay marriage debate was at a fever pitch in Australia. With marriage recently legalized in Washington State, Mike and I decided to secretly elope. The day after Christmas, on the giant Ferris wheel on the Seattle Waterfront, we were married—with Mandy and her family as witnesses and our little bean in utero. Once again, the US had given our emerging family something that our home country could not. We returned to Australia again, this time with photos of our unborn child and two wedding rings, tangible proof that things were finally working out for us.

The next three months dragged. A natural communicator, Mandy sent us daily messages detailing her cravings, her aches and pains, and the occasional spotting (totally normal yet totally terrifying for two guys on the other side of the world). Then, one morning in early April, as she was nearing full-term, this: "I'm feeling cramps, and it feels different than with my first two kids. If you guys want to be here for the birth, you might want to think about coming earlier."

Without hesitation, we moved our tickets and headed to Seattle three weeks earlier than planned. By the time we arrived, the cramping had stopped, so we were left to spend our days in the glorious Seattle spring—strolling the streets, working out at the gym, taking ferries to Bainbridge Island, and working on Australian business hours. In retrospect, it was the ultimate pre-newborn wellness retreat, which was much-needed after the three years of research, planning, travel, and paperwork we had completed to get to this point.

Finally, we were several days past the due date, Mandy was very large, and the doctor recommended we schedule an induction the following morning. After a sleepless night, we drove across that long bridge from Seattle to Bellevue and arrived at Overlake Hospital, our stomachs in knots of antici-pation and uncertainty. We spent the day in Mandy's room, playing *Words with Friends*, texting family members, and waiting for a sign of movement. Although we were assured that it would take most of the day for anything to happen, we felt unable to leave the room for more than a few moments. Finally, at around one a.m., a little girl came screaming into the world at eight pounds, eight ounces, and with a full head of hair. We named her Eleanor.

The following days were a blur of happy exhaustion, new routines, and unfamiliar smells. We stayed in the hospital overnight and eventually took Eleanor back to our rental in the Lower Queen Anne neighborhood. After about a week of sleepless nights and more administrative paperwork—this time passports, and social security and birth certificates—we headed out to the Washington coast for a quiet getaway with Chris, Mandy, and her children. It was a beautiful ending to what turned out to be an idyllic journey.

Then, at just fourteen days old, Eleanor made her first international flight, and we headed home to Melbourne. We felt an immense sense of gratitude to the United States for allowing us to pursue the pathway to parenthood, as well as to legally recognize our relationship through marriage. We had also spent many, many weeks "living" in the US and had come to enjoy the American lifestyle and diversity of thought. Although we never intended to move to the US for good, eighteen months after Eleanor's birth, I was offered the opportunity to transfer to New York with my employer. With Eleanor already a US citizen and Mike and I being married in the US, it seemed a natural coda to our journey to parenthood. In March 2016, we made the move.

Living in New York City has allowed us to see Mandy's family at least once a year, in Seattle, New York, or at a mutual vacation destination. Mandy's children and Eleanor call themselves womb-mates, and as they get older, I'm hopeful they can continue this unique friendship. The physical distance has made it more difficult to maintain a relationship with my cousin Bec, Eleanor's biological mother, but we remain close and chat online regularly, cherishing the visits to Australia where Eleanor can spend some time with her.

In New York City, Eleanor, Mike, and I are surrounded by such a diverse array of family situations that we're rarely reminded that our family origins are, in fact, extraordinary in the true definition of the word. The exception to this,

however, is at the beginning of the school year each
September when Eleanor's new classmates try and piece
together why she doesn't have a mom. As a preteen, she
speaks about it with a sense of pride and bemusement—confident in her birth story, comfortable explaining the wondrous
science that led to her arrival on this planet, and proud of the
"tummy mommy" and "egg mommy" who gave her the vital
ingredients to begin her life.

Without doubt, our path to parenthood has been the most
difficult, challenging, and rewarding thing I have done in my
life—but what parent wouldn't say the same thing? The
immense privilege of having the time and resources to navigate this journey is something I am grateful for every day. I
sometimes wonder: Had I known what would be involved,
would I have had the courage to pursue this path? In those
moments, I need only to look at Eleanor and see the wickedly
funny, laser-smart, supremely confident female who I have the
privilege to know and love. In those moments, I know, without
doubt, that whatever one's path to parenthood, the destination
is always worth the journey.

Discussion Questions

The author and his partner explored many different paths to parenthood before settling on surrogacy. And while their path to starting a family involved some painful, confusing moments, on reflection, he wouldn't change it. Through the process, he also experienced the silver lining of forming unexpected friendships and bonds with the other individuals involved in his "baby-making team."

1. The author discusses his initial discomfort with commercial surrogacy and his worry that it would feel like "renting a womb" instead of an intimate partnership to bring a baby into the world. What are your thoughts and feelings on this topic?
2. The author's daughter refers to her "egg mommy" and her "tummy mommy" when speaking about her family. There are also other cases where children born from the same sperm donor connect and get to know one another. How have modern fertility treatments changed (or how should they change) the way we define *family*?

9

HEARTACHE AND HOPE

SARAH KAMP

The emotions that ran through me when I saw the positive pregnancy test are something I'd never experienced in my life. It was pure happiness followed by the question, *Is this really happening?* I felt on top of the world. It was the last workday before Christmas break, and I spent the day with extra pep in my step. I decided I would tell my husband the next morning before heading out to vacation—that is, if the pregnancy test was still positive the next day.

The next morning, I took a digital test so it would have the word for my husband to see: *pregnant*. As he was getting ready to head out, I said I had a small gift for him before we left. When he saw it, he looked at me with his eyes wide open and the biggest grin I had ever seen. I knew he was experiencing the pure joy I'd felt the day before. Together, we already felt so much love for this life and bundle of joy.

My world was forever changed on August 30, 2019, the day before our due date. A trapdoor opened, and my husband and I fell through it and continued to fall for quite some time. We had just been to an appointment two days earlier where we heard the baby's strong heartbeat and had a membrane sweep. We knew we were days away from our life changing; we would finally be a party of three.

On Friday—the day before the due date—I realized I hadn't felt the baby much, whereas normally I had morning kicks. I tried all the tricks—laid on my side, drank lemonade—but something was different. I remember calling a friend who said I could come over and use her Doppler, but for some reason that did not feel like the right choice. I had flashbacks of every appointment where my doctor had told me that if something felt wrong, I should go straight to labor and delivery. So that's what I did.

My husband met me there, and as we were checked in and wheeled off, I thought I was being over-dramatic. I figured we'd be there for fifteen minutes, long enough to hear the baby on the Doppler and know all was safe. But when the nurse tried the Doppler, there was silence. You could hear a pin drop. We waited while she got the doctor, and my heart dropped. I knew. Looking at my husband's face of confusion, I remember thinking, *The baby is gone.*

The doctor tried the ultrasound, then turned the machine off, sat next to us, and said, "I'm so sorry; there's no heartbeat." Then, there was only continued silence. No "Let's go to the ER and save the baby." That statement is final. Your future—your child—is gone.

This was the first trapdoor; our dreams, our wishes, our envisioned future, gone in one moment.

The second trapdoor was realizing a full-term, forty-week-old baby was inside me and had to come out. I panicked. "I still need to have the baby," I said as tears poured down my face. It felt impossible to breathe. I wanted to scream; I wanted to run and pretend like nothing had happened.

The calls to our parents are a haze, explaining to the people who brought us into the world that their grandchild was gone, that they'd never get to watch them grow. Within minutes, all four grandparents were at the hospital with open arms full of support. After discussions with the nurse and doctor, I elected to have a C-section the next morning.

At this point, there was nothing to do but get in our car and drive home. I stared out the window, crying as I'd continue to do for months to come. That night was silent, full of little sleep and looking out the window at the stars, wondering how and why.

The next morning, we arrived at the hospital at 5:30 a.m. to check in and deliver our baby who was already gone. Entering the emergency room and checking in, I was asked, "What are you here for?" When I said a C-section, the woman excitedly asked if I knew what I was having.

"No," I said as tears silently rolled down my cheeks. I walked back to my husband and sat with my head against the wall. My husband and I were then instructed to walk back to labor and delivery alone—no wheelchair, no assistance, just us and my forty-week belly.

My doctor appeared from around the corner moments before I was wheeled in for the procedure. She had come in on her day off, broken-hearted just like my husband and I were. She had watched us, full of joy for forty weeks as we awaited our first child.

Before the procedure, she warned us there isn't a known cause of stillbirth and asked about the option of autopsy. In less than twelve hours, I had gone from thinking the baby was days away to deciding if we'd do an autopsy. This was not something I'd read about on pregnancy blogs.

The operating room was full of nurses, doctors, and anesthesiologists. I was hunched over the bed, holding a pillow and trembling—not from the temperature, but from the fear of the unknown, from the nightmare I was currently living. The needle going into my back, the sheer pain that didn't exist because it didn't compare. I lay there, waiting to find out if it was a boy or girl. My husband rubbed my arms as I was physically numbed from the waist down. And mentally, I was numb to the world.

When the doctor said, "It's a girl," the emotions that overcame my body were astonishment, pride, joy, and heartbreak. That was the second I realized happiness and sadness could coexist. I got my girl, but at the same moment, I didn't. The dream I had about our years of yelling, "Harper!" in the house, at the beach, and on the basketball court would never happen. She was given to me and taken from me in the same second.

Moments later, we learned the cause: a knot in the umbilical cord.

After forty weeks of carrying my first child, four to five hours was the amount of time we spent with her in our room. There is never enough time, but these minutes were full of love, smiles, and tears. Harper met all four grandparents. We gave her kisses and rocked her endlessly. We did the best we could with the knowledge we had at the time we had it. If I could go back, I'd give her a million more kisses, bathe her for the first time, and dress her in her going-home outfit. I would take off her beanie and unswaddle her to see her toes. Or maybe I would not change a thing, as the memories we have are pure perfection.

Packing up to head home empty-handed and being wheeled to the car with no car seat, no baby cries, and no going-home outfits was our reality. My parents had already removed the car seat. Going home to silence. The stroller was no longer in the family room, the swing was nowhere to be seen, and the signs of an expected baby were hidden behind a closed door. A fully prepared room, ready to be Harper's, now was and wasn't hers.

Those early weeks consisted of staying up way too late with my pillow full of tears, crying in silence and trying not to wake my husband, who, more than likely, was doing the same. It was in the middle of the night when I went to the search bar on Instagram and typed in "stillbirth." It had been a foreign term to me before August 31, 2019. I had never known anyone who had experienced it, and at the age of thirty, I didn't even know it was a possibility. I was completely blindsided when it happened to me, but I knew I could not be alone.

The support I received from the hospital and doctors was virtually nonexistent. Yes, I was given a folder with 1-800 numbers to crisis lines and a website for support, but that was it. That night online, I found a rabbit hole of posts from women and men who knew exactly what I was going through. There were thousands of people sharing their stories, their babies, and their lives with the world through social media. They had built a community to make sure others did not feel alone.

It was through their strength that I decided to do the same. Over time, the bonds I made with those women, most of whom I have never met in person, saved me. They validated my feelings and lent their support and direct messages as a way to connect and share our birth stories and pictures of our babies.

Pregnancy is full of talking about your feelings, your symptoms, the baby, and your future. But what many do not realize is that with the passing of your baby, you don't want your child's memory to also die. The desire to share still exists, the birth still happened, the time with your baby happened, and the memories are there. Find the people who support you and allow you to feel less alone. Find the men and women who grieve and experience their loss in a similar way, who you can connect with and feel comfort from.

For the first few months after Harper's death, I experienced anxiety and panic attacks. Often they were brought on by everyday activities or things others wouldn't necessarily see as "triggers." For example, after my C-section, all the seams from my yoga pants fell directly on my scar, making them impossible to wear. The easy solution was to go to the mall and buy myself a pair of nice pants that I'd feel good in, so off to Lululemon I went.

I went three times, driving twenty minutes there and back each time only to sit in the parking lot without the courage to leave the car. Each time I thought, *What if I see someone? What will I say? How do I talk to the associate in the store? Do I tell them I just gave birth two weeks ago, but the baby is dead and the weight is gone?* It felt impossible to go back into a social environment and subject myself to the unknown.

Looking back, I was in protection mode, sheltering myself from others and their thoughts—something I would continue to do for years to come. The most minute tasks became mountains to climb. Nevertheless, on my fourth attempt, I persisted, walking through the mall to find two pairs of pants that I would learn to live in during the coming months. My palms were sweaty, but I had survived my first solo outing.

Many times, we hide our pain because others don't know how to handle it, the responses are something we can't handle, or we are tired of comforting other people in their feelings about our story.

Checking out at Trader Joe's, I saw the doctor who had held the unwanted job of telling me my baby was gone. I was so excited to see him in the wild. To this day, I believe the compassion and empathy he showed my husband and me is one of the reasons we made it through. After he left, the clerk asked how I knew him. I panicked and decided for the first time I'd tell my truth.

"He delivered my daughter last month," I said. "Unfortunately, she was stillborn due to a knot in the umbilical cord."

"Oh, my son had a knot too," the clerk responded. "It was scary. He's eighteen."

Dagger to the heart. I already knew the stats on knots, and how common they are and how unlikely they are to cause a death. So this broke me. *Why would you tell me this?* I wondered.

Why do we try to compare and find something similar that we feel will comfort the grieving?

With the balloons, food, friends, and family, birthdays are a big deal, especially for children. But the anticipation of your dead child's birthday comes with many mixed emotions. *How do I honor my baby? Do I celebrate? Mourn? Stay home alone? Include others? Will I be OK?* There are no clear answers, and the days leading up to this milestone are different for each person. We chose to celebrate. We'd never had a funeral, so it felt like we had never gotten to celebrate the life we had created. And while that life may have been short, she had lived those forty weeks inside of me.

Shopping was a mixed bag of emotions. I sought out the self-checkout so as not to encounter a clerk asking about the decor and the extra-large, gold foil balloon shaped like the number one. It was refreshing to buy all the things I would have if Harper had been there—the pink tablecloths, napkins, silverware, and balloons. I felt like a mom.

Due to COVID, we limited the party to our immediate family and held it outdoors; but it was perfect. Harper's nieces released balloons with letters to heaven. Harper's ombré pink cake was cut after Steve and I blew out her candle. It was a special day—one I'd never imagined, but one that we needed.

It's been two years—six-hundred-plus days—and the box from the first pregnancy test I purchased, a two-pack, is still in the cabinet with one remaining test. Here I am, a year later, without a baby in my arms and still working on trying to conceive a sibling. The journey of trying to conceive has entirely new meaning when your first pregnancy ends in death. The blissful innocence you once had no longer exists. And no matter how hard others try to understand, they just cannot unless they have been through your situation.

At my first visit to a therapist after we lost Harper, the counselor asked within the first ten minutes if we were trying again. At this point, it had been two months since I'd lost my daughter. I was in no shape to try again. This question stung me to my core. I thought, *Why are you asking me if I'm trying again? I didn't try and fail; my child died. I came to therapy to focus on Harper, so why are we talking about the unconceived next baby?*

This brings up the idea, which is so often spewed on moms who've lost a child, that another baby will heal your broken heart. Babies do not replace babies. A second baby will be a baby with a missing sister. A second baby will be the constant reminder that you missed crucial milestones with your first. A second baby, for me, will mean being a second first-time mom, because I don't know what it is like to raise a child, to breast-feed, to wake up to cries.

At my post-op checkup, Steve and I sat in the room, crying with our doctor. All three of us hurt; all three of us knew Harper should have been at that appointment. She had been a healthy, perfect baby; her umbilical cord was not. We were left empty, wanting more.

When we asked our doctor when we could start trying to conceive again, thinking the answer would be around six months, our hearts sank when she told us my body needed a year to heal. I was in great shape, had no complications with the pregnancy, but a year was what we decided. It broke my heart, but it also allowed me to focus on Harper.

I spent a year honoring Harper's monthly milestones, sitting in my thoughts, seeking therapy, learning my boundaries. It was a year I did not ask for, but a year that I truly needed. I don't say this to imply everyone should wait a year but to tell you that if you are in the waiting period or are not ready yet to conceive, that is OK. You are allowed to have time to focus on your feelings, the bond you had with your child, and the bond you continue to form. Giving myself the year allowed me to fully be in a place of understanding.

While no baby's life should be cut short, I understand this is my life now, and that is OK. Harper may not physically be here, but she will always be here as a part of our family. She plays a role in what we do and how we live our lives moving forward.

———

Discussion Questions

The author lost her daughter to stillbirth but chose to honor her at her first birthday with a celebration of the short time they'd had together. She also chose to take her time before trying to conceive again, with the understanding that she needed it to honor Harper and the fact that "babies don't replace babies." Instead of avoiding talking about her experience, she welcomed it into her life with the acknowledgment that the daughter she will never raise is still a part of their family and will always play a role in their lives.

1. The author mentions how when faced with other people's grief, people often find the need to compare their own experience, despite the fact that they will never understand. Why do you think people have this instinct?

2. At her first visit with a therapist after her daughter's death, the author was immediately asked if she was trying to conceive again. She says this "brings up the idea, which is so often spewed on moms who've lost a child, that another baby will heal your broken heart." Why do you think this happens?

10

INSTANTLY INFERTILE

DR. CARLI BLAU

There's a classic song about not getting what you want but instead getting what you need. I'd like to propose an update to this, because I believe the most profound and influential life lessons come not from getting what we want when we desire it, but rather from handling those disappointments and persevering through them.

As a teenager, my periods became heavy, causing me to miss school often because of cramps. And when I started having sex with my boyfriend at age fourteen, sex became painful too. A few years later, my doctor became suspicious that I had endometriosis, a gynecological disease in which tissue similar to the tissue found in the lining of the uterus grows outside of the uterus where it doesn't belong. The tissue adheres to other organs causing pain, inflammation, and discomfort. As my physician began to monitor my symptoms, I knew I might need surgery to address this condition. And more frightening to me, I learned that endometriosis could lead to infertility.

At that time, my impression was that infertility would mean I might not be able to have children. The horror! I had wanted to be a mother since the day I came into the world. As a child, I carried around my dolls, Jonathan and Samantha, and told people I had birthed them. So when I learned that something like endometriosis could potentially make me unable to bear children, I felt like a captain who sees a storm brewing above the sea.

The thing about dark clouds is when we see them, we know a storm is coming. We may not know when or if a deluge will hit us, but we know the darker the cloud, the more damaging the storm. After much pain, heavy bleeding, and painful intercourse—despite intervention with hormonal birth control and naproxen sodium—I had surgery and got a confirmed diagnosis of endometriosis. On the day I was officially diagnosed, I began to sense the dark cloud of infertility over my head. And like anyone else without an umbrella, I began to fear it.

Later, at twenty-five years young and within minutes of finishing sex with Ryan, my then-boyfriend and now husband, I became violently sick—the kind of sick that you're embarrassed for someone else to see. My ears began to ring, the cramps swarmed in, and I vomited and had diarrhea at the same time. *Hot*, I know. When my boyfriend checked on me in the bathroom and found me drenched in sweat, he held me up by the bun on my head until my nausea stopped.

"That's when the next phase of our relationship began," I jokingly told him later, "because at that point, you had seen too much *not* to become the man I married."

This episode was followed by another appointment with my endometriosis surgeon. Ryan came with me, and the doctor told us both that my condition looked serious. If I wanted to have children, I'd probably have to start earlier rather than later to avoid the need for reproductive treatment.

We were twenty-five and twenty-six, holding hands in the back of a New York City yellow taxi in the hot summer heat, when I told him, "I will always love you, but if this is not something you're ready for, I'd understand if you want to end this now before it gets more serious."

We've now been together for more than a decade.

My doctors told me to stay on birth control until we were ready to start trying because it would help keep my endometriosis at bay. So when we got married, my gift to myself was the choice to stop taking the pill. I've always been one to get what I want when I want it, not because it's just handed to me, but because I work for it. At this point, I was prepared to work for pregnancy and motherhood. Also, as a sex therapist, I knew the amount of sex that would be needed to get there, and thanks to sexual chemistry, I wasn't afraid to "do the work."

Month after month, my period didn't come. I had a withdrawal bleed a few weeks after stopping the pill and then nothing. Crickets. I'd ovulate once every two to three months in no specific pattern. My cycles ranged from thirty-five to ninety days. The more time passed, the more defeated I felt. And let's call a spade a spade; sex is fun at first when you're trying to conceive and enjoying the intimacy of it, but it doesn't take long before the love is lost and the distance between you and the person you want to make a baby with begins.

Despite all my education and training in reproductive biology as a women's health expert and sex therapist, I didn't know it could take a year or more for my body to regulate after coming off hormonal birth control. This is why they say there is value to both an education in school and life experience. The nuances around the attempt and desire to get pregnant are not spoken about. Nor is education provided to women who want to get pregnant on how to do it—and this is a shame.

I came to learn that it also takes a few months of tracking consistent cycles to develop an understanding of when ovulation takes place. Some women who have a twenty-eight- to thirty-five-day cycle ovulate early, some ovulate late, and while there are averages, each woman's individual body is completely unique. Despite all this, instead of being told that I needed a year off the pill to let my body regulate, I got the recommendation to stay on the pill so my endometriosis wouldn't get worse. I was also told that I could use reproductive interventions like medicated cycles or fertility treatment if needed.

What we don't tell women, however, is that these treatments are not guaranteed. And thus begins a woman's experience with infertility.

After eight months of consistent sex, inconsistent cycles, and irregular ovulation, I began to fear the big I-word. If it walks like a duck, quacks like a duck, and looks like a duck, it's a duck, right? Well, when it comes to infertility, if you don't ovulate, you have irregular cycles, and conception never occurs despite regular sex, then you are screwed.

Ryan and I quickly surrendered to fertility treatment. I felt such pressure to get the ball rolling—driven by fear that if I didn't begin immediately, I could potentially not conceive. I was afraid that the older I got, the smaller my chance of conception would become. So without hesitation, I went through three rounds of Clomid with timed intercourse, three rounds of letrozole with trigger shots, a chemical pregnancy at six weeks, and an intrauterine insemination. Nine months later, nothing had worked, and I was furious. After so much medical intervention, how was it that with so much control, I still had none?

That's the thing about infertility treatment that no one prepares women for. We can use every medical intervention and manage every aspect of our lives, but when it comes down to it, the true birth within ourselves as mothers occurs in recognizing we really have no control. In our journey to motherhood, our safety for ourselves—and ultimately for our children—doesn't come through what we control, but through our ability to remain stable in the face of what we can't control.

As I furthered my education, pursuing a doctorate in clinical sex therapy, I studied what I was interested in: infertility and sex—specifically, the relationship between infertility-related sexual stress and sexual esteem. Through my studies, I began to dissect what it means to be infertile. In doing so, I learned that existing literature includes sixteen different definitions of infertility. So despite women all over the world being scared into fertility treatment, there is no single, universal definition for the word *infertility*.

The World Health Organization (WHO) splits the different definitions into categories: clinical, demographic, epidemiological, and socially constructed. There is also primary and secondary infertility, as well as infertility as a disability.

The problem here is that when studying anything, a universal definition is imperative for obtaining results that can bring about change. Not having that is like trying to solve the most complicated math problem without ever finding a common denominator—near impossible.

This led me to wonder what definition fertility clinics and reproductive doctors use when determining if someone is infertile, or how they determine when to begin treating them as if they are. And while I understand how labels can be confining, when it comes to fertility, infertility, and the journey to motherhood, not having clear definitions leaves room for further confusion. It also leads to a lack of consistency and reliability among research, medical data, and policies, and most importantly, treatment.

This confusion and ambiguity about the definition of infertility often compounds our fear of it while also contributing to our desire to identify with it. Because if we identify as infertile, we gain some faux sense of control. We associate infertility with treatment options and a hope for success based on reproductive technology, even though these mechanisms are merely options, not solutions.

While having something to identify with can be empowering for some, it can be defeating for others. After doing multiple tries with IUI and timed intercourse, which failed and led to one miscarriage, I did one retrieval and one round of IVF to conceive my daughter. I had some complications along the way, including a cyst, but nonetheless my pregnancy was successful.

As someone who later got pregnant with my second child naturally without trying, I will still say getting pregnant is not easy! Biologically speaking, conception and pregnancy are multifaceted and extremely complex. Many moving parts must come together simultaneously and serendipitously for conception to occur. You therefore don't need to be deemed broken if you don't conceive after one year. Nor should you be scared into treatment because of another condition.

If you self-identify as infertile out of fear before you have a medical and historical reason to, please be mindful of the mental repercussions of that choice. In a study published in 1993, the psychological symptoms of infertile women were compared to patients who had other chronic medical conditions. Infertile women were found to have global symptom scores equivalent to patients suffering from cancer, cardiac rehabilitation, and hypertension (A.D. Domar, P.C. Zuttermeister, R. Friedman, "The Psychological Impact of Infertility: A Comparison with Patients with Other Medical Conditions," *J Psychosom Obstet Gynaecol*).

We are gifted with a beautiful community on social media and an internet full of like-minded women who want to be mothers yet share the fear of never getting there. As you view their stories, it's also worth remembering that your journey is your own, and that no one else in this world will share it. Your story is not someone else's, and someone else's nightmare does not have to be your future. Think about it like this: Imagine you need glasses. If you're wearing lenses that are meant for someone else, you won't see the world clearly. Chances are you'll also do damage to your eyes while wearing a prescription meant for someone else. Social media can sometimes force us to look through a lens that doesn't work for us.

As a sex therapist and educator, I see a need for comprehensive sex ed about how to get pregnant, including teaching women when to come off hormonal contraceptives and maybe even encouraging condom use instead of hormonal contraception so they can learn about their cycles and bodies. Of course, there are women like me with diagnoses like endometriosis or polycystic ovary syndrome (PCOS) who thus may be instructed to remain on hormonal contraceptives. But I do wonder, if I had come off the pill years before trying to conceive and given my body a chance to work with me, whether I would have needed the intense treatment I went through. We'll never know. Either way, I do hope that my research can encourage women to learn about their bodies first, as it may save them from the mental, physical, and sexual struggle that comes with identifying as infertile.

We live in a society that values solutions to problems rather than education to avoid them. Can you imagine the gravity of our success if women were merely taught how to get pregnant? If getting pregnant were as easy as a man and woman having sex, fertility clinics would not be booming, and I wouldn't be as busy as a sex therapist. The truth is, we pathologize the problem and make money by finding solutions instead of empowering people through education to avoid these issues.

Motherhood may be achievable if we infuse our journey with empowerment and education around getting to know our own bodies and what they need to get pregnant. Believing our body can work with us, instead of deciding it is working against us, can bring wonders.

There's a saying, "She believed she could, so she did." In

all my research, I have concluded that we find strength when we believe in ourselves. We thus have a duty to ourselves to be informed in order to give our bodies the tools they need to conceive *before* we convince ourselves we're infertile. Our souls deserve that chance, and it's up to us to take it.

To you, your journey, and the battle many of us have or will have: You've got this; we've got this.

———

Discussion Questions

The author believes we should take more care and consideration in how we apply the label of infertility, and that women could avoid a lot of angst by learning about how their bodies work before rushing to fertility interventions. She celebrates the idea of thinking of our bodies as something that can work *for* us instead of against us, if we educate and empower ourselves with knowledge about how they work.

1. Have you ever been in a situation where you felt that your body failed you? How did you handle it? Who and what did you depend on to get through it?
2. The author makes the point that while social media can help us find a community, it also introduces the danger of overidentifying with other people's stories instead of charting our own paths. How have you experienced this? In what ways do you find social media to be a place of community or of comparison?

11

EMBRACING THE UNEXPECTED GIFT

NICOLE NYBERG

"Nicole, you had a little boy." These are words I had always dreamt of hearing, but not under the circumstances in which they occurred. Growing up, I had always dreamed of getting married and having children. From a very young age, I loved children—especially babies. So it was not a surprise to anyone that my ultimate career goal was to work in neonatology within a neonatal intensive care unit, or NICU.

Working in the NICU was everything I had hoped for and more. I had a lot to learn, but I had found my calling. And while I loved being a bedside nurse in the NICU, I wanted to do more. So I decided to go further and apply to graduate school to become a neonatal nurse practitioner, or NNP. Midway through my program, I met my future husband, and after a quick courtship we became engaged. The following year was a whirlwind: We bought a house and moved, I graduated with my master of science in nursing, we got married, and I passed my boards and became a board-certified NNP.

I was already on the older side, so once we were married, we did not delay our attempt to start our family. Luckily, within a couple of months, I became pregnant. We were beyond ecstatic. My first trimester of the pregnancy moved along seamlessly. I would talk to the baby and journal to him or her trying to cherish every moment. I was so worried about a possible miscarriage that when the first trimester ended, I was relieved it had gone well. I could finally breathe.

But a couple of weeks into my second trimester, I started to experience some bleeding. I remember getting on my knees and praying to God that my baby would be OK. Eventually the bleeding dissipated, but a few days later during my orientation as a new NNP, I felt some uncomfortable tightness in my abdomen. I went to see my doctor and found out I was consistently contracting. I was placed on bed rest at home, but I ended up in the hospital that evening due to preterm labor at just fifteen weeks.

My obstetrician treated me with medications to stop the contractions, which helped, and with his approval I returned to work. But that came to an abrupt halt one evening when I again began to bleed. As I drove to the hospital, I was relieved to feel the baby kick. At eighteen weeks, my little one was trying to reassure me.

After spending the night in the hospital, I was again placed on strict bed rest at home. I felt utterly powerless, and despite my lack of activity, the bleeding continued for the next several weeks. Luckily, however, we were constantly reassured by the baby's activity and movement. Personally and professionally, it was a frightening time full of uncertainty. Despite my body trying to fail me, I was doing everything in my power to keep our baby safe and growing inside me.

Then one day, I collapsed at home due to such significant bleeding. My husband, Josh, scooped me off the floor, put me in the car, and sped me to the local hospital. I was twenty-three weeks pregnant. They were able to stabilize me and stop the contractions, but I was kept as an inpatient for observation while they considered moving me to a hospital with a higher level of care. Since I had stabilized, however, they ultimately opted to wait.

Josh started to head home for the night despite my pleas for him to stay. When he was halfway down the hall, I called to him, crying and begging him to come back. He did return for a while, but in the end, he still went home.

Sadly, my maternal instincts were right. At the stroke of midnight, my nurse woke me up to use the restroom in hopes that my new onset of contractions were due to a full bladder. But instead, a sharp pain suddenly shot across my abdomen— a feeling that persisted and filled me with a growing unease.

My obstetrician soon arrived and confirmed that the baby's heart rate was dropping. They would need to do an emergency cesarean section.

Without Josh present, they rushed me back to the operating room. On my way, I frantically called the on-call NNP at the hospital where I worked, which I knew had a better equipped NICU. I let her know that I was going to have the baby and needed her to send a transport team to take the baby to their hospital. In absolute shock, all she could utter was, "I'm sorry. I'm so sorry."

In the OR, the chaos continued. Without the fetal heart rate monitor in place, I cried to my nurse because we did not know if there was still a heartbeat. She paused, found a Doppler, and placed it on my abdomen. We both breathed a sigh of relief to hear the beautiful sound of my sweet baby's heart beating away. I was fearful that it would be the last time I would hear the heartbeat of our child, since I presumed our extremely premature baby would not survive the delivery.

Dealing with the Aftermath

I woke up to, "Nicole, you had a little boy—and he is doing OK." Our baby was still alive! Even amidst my grogginess, I will never forget those words. William Russell Nyberg was born at twenty-three weeks, weighing one pound, six ounces. Unfortunately, the odds were against him.

As soon as I was well enough, they rolled me in to see William. Prior to his delivery, I had joked with the nurses that if necessary, I would crawl across my bed to intubate him. Unfortunately, despite my son desperately needing my expertise, I was incredibly nauseous after being under general anesthesia. I felt utterly helpless. I could barely wrap my head around what had just happened, let alone help my son. As his mother, my only job was to protect him while he was growing inside of me. But now here he was, helpless in the outside world, and I was still unable to protect him.

He was not intubated, so we could hear his little attempts to cry. I tried to verbally guide the nurses and respiratory therapists, since I was unable to physically help. Josh had arrived, and the anesthesiologist told my husband he was unsure how I was even awake, let alone able to lie next to William on my stretcher and hold his tiny hand. My maternal strength was greater than any medication they had given me.

I will never forget seeing the transport team from my hospital walk through the door. Once they arrived, I was finally able to lie back, take a breath, and rest. They immediately intubated him, warmed him up, and prepared him for his transport. To see William leave was so incredibly difficult. I did not know if I would ever see him alive again.

We sent my sister-in-law, Amanda—a family nurse practitioner—to stay with William and be the eyes and ears for us. We were blessed by her presence and that of a fellow NNP, Lisa, who took turns sitting with William. They updated us for the first couple of days until we could get there to be with him.

William was in very critical condition and required a blood transfusion and several other interventions early on. The neonatologist recommended a head ultrasound to see if William was experiencing an intraventricular hemorrhage or bleeding in the ventricles in his brain. We were immediately catapulted into the intense NICU world that I knew so well but never anticipated I would experience as a parent.

I was finally able to be discharged, and I traveled to be with William. As I walked into the NICU for the first time to see my son, I felt like a stranger walking into what previously had been such a familiar place. I will never forget stepping up to see William in his Isolette full of glowing blue lights from all his phototherapy. Although his eyes were still fused closed and he wore eye shields, I saw the cutest little nose I had ever seen.

Holding Dual Identities

I quickly discovered that while I had been propelled into a familiar world, I knew it only from a singular point of view. You never really know something in its entirety unless you have experienced it from all angles. Now, not only was I experiencing the NICU as a parent but as a parent of a twenty-three-weeker. To make matters worse, I now had to balance my role as a mother of a critically ill baby in the NICU with that of my status as an NNP whose coworkers were caring for William.

Whereas most NICU parents are apprehensive to touch their premature baby or jump in to help, I certainly was not! I immediately assisted in any way I could. I decided to have him baptized when he was five days old because we were unsure what the future held for him. That was also the first day I was able to do skin-to-skin or kangaroo care with him. To hold my son and be reconnected with him was the best feeling in the world. Then, when William was nine days old, he finally opened his eyes. What a beautiful sight!

We had visitors come to see William, and prayers were being lifted for him from coast to coast. I had never felt such an outpouring of love and support in my whole life. William was changing lives and had people who had never prayed before on their knees praying. I was amazed at how someone so tiny could promote so much change, positivity, and goodness.

Yet despite all this, I felt as though I was walking on eggshells. While William was doing remarkably well for a twenty-three-weeker, I knew too much about what could go wrong in the typical NICU journey to get comfortable.

In spite of our support, I had never felt so alone. I completely shut out the world around us. I put on a good show for everyone, but I typically refused offers of rides and meals to avoid repeating the same questions and typical conversations. Friends, family, and acquaintances knew my profession, so for any other NICU baby, I would have been the one they turned to with questions—and I still was. But how could I objectively answer their questions when the subject matter was my son? Everything was different now. I didn't want to answer how he was doing, because I knew that it could all change in a heartbeat. I didn't want to explain the plan of care and what to expect, because this was not just any patient; it was my son. And I certainly did not want to try and predict what may lie ahead, because I was too superstitious and afraid that it would all go downhill if I did.

Feeling Alone Together

I rarely left William's side or traveled home, opting instead to stay with my brother and sister-in-law who lived closer to the hospital. Josh came to visit William on the weekends and occasionally after work during the week. Early on, I noticed Josh wasn't coming to the hospital much, and he later admitted he was afraid of getting too attached to William.

Josh and I endured individual struggles but didn't discuss them. We also handled our grief very differently. I remember the chaplain talking to us at William's bedside; I told her I was scared that William wasn't going to live and that I didn't know how I would survive it. Josh sat there all brave and positive, and in that moment, I wanted to slap him. I now understand he was trying to stay positive for me, but it was very difficult and eye-opening to see how differently we handled our individual grief and trauma.

Any couple with a sick child will endure an immense amount of stress. Sadly, there is no ample preparation for a parent to see their child struggle and fight to live. And added to this, Josh and I were newlyweds and really just getting to know each other. We had been thrown a massive curveball that we were absolutely not prepared to handle, individually or together.

As a couple, we were apart most days. I sat with William and stayed in town while Josh stayed at home, attempting to work and be with my eight-year-old stepdaughter. I wanted him to be at the NICU more, and he wanted me home more. But I was not going to leave William's side. To see him fighting day in and day out with such strength, determination, and courage rocked my soul. With all the uphill battles he had to climb, the least I could do was sit with him, hold him, read to him, pump breastmilk for him, sing to him, and pray with him. And if, God forbid, William was taken from us, I did not want to have one regret about the time I'd spent with him while he was in the NICU, fighting for his life so bravely.

When I was present, I helped the nurses and gently contained William during his care times. Sadly, there were several moments when he needed extra breaths from the ventilator due to heart rate drops or desaturations. In those moments, all I could do was stand there, praying and willing him to come back. The internal struggle I faced each day was agonizing, as I wanted to stay in my lane as his mother but also knew, as an NNP, what interventions were needed. I had to resist the urge to give extra breaths, adjust his oxygen, or step in before the nurses, which was one of the hardest things I'd ever done. And I'd be remiss if I said I never stepped in or quietly told the nurses I'd take over if needed.

As William progressed, it was time to begin weaning him from the ventilator. And although I knew, as an NNP, that the first attempt might not be successful, my heart still ached when he had to be reintubated. The anguish and helplessness I felt as a parent seeing William struggle and undergo treatments due to his terrible skin breakdown, IV attempts, heel sticks, and re-securement of his breathing tube is indescribable. Although I knew all the procedures were necessary, it was incredibly difficult to stand there helplessly and watch my son experience them. One day, I wrote in my journal, "If I could take on all of your pain and anguish, I would in a heartbeat."

Witnessing a Miracle

We had unexpected gifts sent to us from friends I hadn't heard from in years. Amanda's and Lisa's willingness to sit with William in the first few days when we couldn't be there was unforgettable. On some nights, my brother and sister-in-law would insist that I go home, and they would have a date night at William's bedside or sit and pray with him individually so I could rest. In addition to allowing me to stay in their home, they also came up with his nickname, Strong-Willed. Nurses took pictures of William when he hit milestones like opening his eyes or when he did something adorable, which was often. One of the neonatologists would either call or come visit us even on his days off. We were given a sweet william plant from a nurse, plus gift cards, monetary gifts, and so much more from so many friends and family members.

The biggest reward we experienced along William's NICU journey was witnessing firsthand his bravery, willpower, strength, and multitude of daily successes. We were afforded the blessing of observing a miracle in the making right before our very eyes. If I had not been there to see for myself, I absolutely would not have believed it.

After William stabilized and became two months old, I decided to go back to work. So, ironically, I practiced as an NNP in the NICU where William was a patient so I could save the last month of my maternity leave for when he came home. To say it was surreal to be working in the unit where my child was a current patient does not even begin to capture it. While our care team did rounds on the other patients, I acted as the NNP; then at William's bedside, I reverted to my maternal role. I remember the day of one of his eye exams when they came to find me on the unit because he was having so many heart rate drops. I struggled to successfully fill each role—a challenge that proved impossible.

After ninety-one days, we brought William home. It was a glorious day! He was on oxygen and monitors, but he was home. I don't remember a lot from those early days. I'm unsure if I was dealing with postpartum depression or post-traumatic stress disorder (PTSD). I did know, though, how incredibly lucky we were to not only have William home, but that he was so healthy overall. So even if I was feeling down, I wasn't going to talk to anyone about it. Because how could I be sad? Our twenty-three-week miracle had just survived his NICU journey and was home with us.

Partly, I hadn't allowed myself to really feel during his time in the NICU either. I was so focused on William and his success that I shoved down any other feeling that crept up. As a mother of a NICU baby, you conjure up fortitude from a place within that you never knew existed. I had an internal will to push through even when I thought I could not any more. I never had time to absorb what had just happened—including all the emotions that should have surrounded it—because I had moved on to survival mode for my baby.

Now the guilt, on the other hand—I absolutely felt all the guilt. If amidst a conversation a nurse would suggest that William was delivered prematurely because he just couldn't wait to come out and meet us, I would quickly snap back and let them know that it was absolutely not his fault; it was mine. My body had failed me; but most importantly, it had failed him.

When I filled out the postpartum depression survey at my six-week postpartum checkup, I knew exactly how to answer the questions so I could get out of there without any red flags. Even if I had some of the feelings listed, I was not going to acknowledge them. To take the time for more follow-ups and possibly be placed on medication was not an option. I had to get back to the NICU to be with William.

And although I had shut out most of the world while William was in the NICU, I'd still experienced the peace and comfort of the nurses and care team there with me. They became part of our family and William's biggest cheerleaders. We would chat throughout the day, and they were always quick to brag on William, which we loved to hear. When you're in the NICU, all you think about is getting your baby home. But you don't realize that once you're home, your NICU community with whom you've spent months is no longer there. One of your biggest support systems is gone, and once you're home, it's a very isolating time. I didn't fully understand this until I went through it myself.

I spent one full month at home with William before I had to go back to work. I returned part-time, and Josh and our nanny cared for William while I worked.

Wiliam was closely followed and evaluated by a slew of doctors and continued to amaze us with his strength, resiliency, and determination. He came off oxygen completely after being home for a month. He started rolling over at seven months (or what would have been three months, had he been born at full term) and walking at eighteen (or fourteen) months. Other than some fine motor and gross motor struggles, William always rose to the occasion during his evaluations, surprising most of his therapists.

Looking Toward the Future

Josh and I knew we wanted more children, but the possibility of repeating anything similar to my pregnancy with William, his preterm delivery, and the time in the NICU was incredibly scary. We consulted our obstetrician who ultimately sent us to a specialist. After a visit, we were given the green light to move forward in our attempts to expand our family.

As with William's pregnancy, the conception was not the difficult part. Also, eerily, my first trimester was perfectly smooth just like with William. Then, just before I reached fourteen weeks, I started spotting again, and that night I developed a significant, constant pain around my abdomen. The next morning, I woke up and knew that I was contracting. I let Josh and my doctor know, and we were told to head to the hospital.

Once there, I had a conversation with God. I told him plainly that if this pregnancy was heading down the same path as it had with William—with bed rest and an extremely premature delivery—that I could not do it again. I believe I even said that I would rather the pregnancy end at that point than repeat another long, stressful pregnancy and NICU journey. At that moment, I could not fathom how I could be on bed rest while I had William, who was twenty-one months old. And if we had another extremely premature delivery, I knew the unlikely odds that it would end as well as William's journey had.

The contractions ended but picked back up with a vengeance later that evening, and then they couldn't be stopped. After hours of continuous contractions, I felt a trickle of a warm liquid down my leg. It was over. My body had failed me and the baby again.

Just then, my night nurse walked in, and I felt as though an angel had entered the room. It was Susan, the same labor and delivery nurse I'd had the night William was born. The same nurse who paused amongst all the chaos to let me hear William's heartbeat one last time before they put me to sleep.

And suddenly, after hours of contractions, they went away. Upon checking me, Susan could feel the baby had slid down, and she asked me to gently push. And out came this beautiful, perfect, little, tiny baby boy.

Susan was so amazing, and I'll never forget how she oohed and aahed over how adorable he was. You would have never thought that he was a tiny fourteen-week baby by her reaction. He was just under two ounces of teeny, tiny perfection. He had William's beautiful little nose and the most perfect body with tiny fingers and toes.

We had some friends and family come to support us and meet Weston Glenn Nyberg. We took pictures of him, and he stayed in the room with us that night. All my pain medication had finally kicked in, and I was in a dreamlike world. I sang to Weston and read him books that I knew by heart in the middle of the night, as I tried to keep his perfect little body etched in my memory forever. We had to let them take him the next morning, and saying goodbye was incredibly difficult. I had visitors and seemed so rational in our conversations. The staff told me about support groups, but I politely declined. I thought I was fine. And then I went home.

For me, the reality set in later at home when I looked up at our family picture on the wall. Weston would not be in our family picture, ever. Since I didn't want William to see me upset, I went up to our closet and bawled. Josh eventually found me crying on the floor of the closet.

Flowers, visitors, gifts, and condolences came—again, we felt a lot of love and support. We decided to have Weston cremated, and I remember driving to the funeral home and feeling sick. *This is not happening,* I told myself. We had a lovely memorial service for Weston in our home, surrounded by family and friends.

Finally Grieving

I tried to move on from the pain. But I was sad. So, so sad. This was my fault—again. *Why didn't I go in sooner? Why did I make that deal with God? Why was I so quickly willing to give up on my baby? I could have handled it. We would have figured it out. What is wrong with me and my body that it is rejecting these beautiful babies?*

Later that summer, I found out I was pregnant again. We were both shocked and scared. I was so hopeful and cautiously optimistic that this pregnancy was going to be different. Perhaps God had given us an unexpected gift. And while my hormone levels were low initially, we were able to hear a heartbeat at six weeks. But at my next appointment with my obstetrician, he paused—and then paused some more before speaking.

"I am so sorry, Nicole, but there is not a heartbeat anymore."

Why? Why was I given the perception of hope that we had another chance, only for it to all be taken away—again? We weren't even sure if we were going to try again, so I presumed that we had been given an unexpected but beautiful gift. *Why?*

We both knew that we were done trying to have more biological children. We were not going to keep putting ourselves through this horrible pain. So the day after we found out about our loss, we signed Josh up for a vasectomy and chose to officially close that chapter of our lives.

But is it ever really closed? For me, I feel as though we were robbed of our choices. Yes, we chose to no longer attempt to have biological children, but we also felt as though our hand was forced. For the well-being of my mental health, our marriage, and our family, we could not continue to endure this pain.

Again, we moved on.

But being the busy working woman and mother that I was, I never allowed myself the proper time to heal and get the help I desperately needed after our experience with William and other losses.

A few years later, I finally broke down to Josh and realized I needed to talk to someone. So I started to see a therapist and slowly worked through my grief.

"We never move beyond our grief, but we try to find healthy ways to move through life with it," she said to me one day.

This is so true. Whether it is PTSD, trauma, or loss, those experiences will always be with us. They will follow us into our relationships and daily life, but if we can find healthy ways to work through them and manage them, then we are on the right track.

Finding Hope

I'm slowly getting there, but it takes a lot of work and acceptance. I'm not sure if I will ever fully accept the loss of our two babies or understand why they occurred. I continue to try to work through my jealousy, anger, sadness, and unanswered questions. Although I admit to angry moments with God, I still have strong faith. And God has allowed me to see the glory of William despite all the additional pain we endured. What a gift our son has been and continues to be. To witness one of God's miracles right before our eyes is just that, a gift.

I have continued my work as an NNP, spending nearly seven years in the very same NICU where William received most of his ninety-one days of intensive care. Some days, it's not easy. Emergent cesarean sections bother me. Any death in the NICU is of course difficult on its own, but also because I feel an extra twinge of guilt. *Why did that family lose their child? What was so different about William? Will anyone ever know how beyond blessed we feel we are to have William?*

If I'm the provider at extremely preterm deliveries of twenty-three- and twenty-four-weekers, I can put on my professional hat and fully perform my job duties, but it is not without an incredible amount of internal struggle and strength to get through it each time. I have moments of sadness and—I hate to admit it—also jealousy when friends, coworkers, or acquaintances are pregnant. Of course, I am thrilled for them and only wish the best for their families. But it is hard because I continue to feel as though my choices were stripped from me. Even beautiful moments at work after a birth can be difficult. Witnessing joyful, tearful parents as their chubby, full-term baby is placed on the mother's chest after an uneventful delivery is difficult because Josh and I were not able to have that experience. But as the years pass and we continue to delight in William and all of his successes, I can now look back and embrace our NICU experience as the unexpected gift of perspective. It's not an experience I would wish on anyone, but it has changed me to the core, personally and professionally.

Every NICU journey is different, but one thing is certain: You do not forget it, and you will never be the same after it. My hope is that my gift of perspective will not only help NICU families while I'm at work but will also be shared through my advocacy, support, and the education I provide by speaking at conferences, on social media, and through our *Empowering NICU Parents' Podcast.* Our experiences allowed me to discover a new life purpose that has filled me with hope.

Josh and I endured so much stress and anguish early in our marriage, and although it wasn't easy, we are now stronger for it, individually and as a couple. And my son is my hero. The strength, determination, and resilience that William, now eleven years old, has shown is awe-inspiring. He continues to be incredibly "Strong-Willed" and stubborn, but he also has an amazing heart and is incredibly kind, loving, and funny.

I'm thankful he does not remember his initial life experiences. But we do proudly talk to him and remind him how much he has accomplished and just how far he has come. He knows that he was a teeny, teeny, tiny baby who fought for his life and came out all the stronger for it—with just a few scars. He is incredible.

I also openly share the story of our losses to bring more awareness to pregnancy and infant loss. We continue to honor and remember our other babies in our home and daily lives. We have two beautiful angels watching over us who I look forward to holding again one day. My hope is that by openly sharing our experience and its impact on me, it will ultimately help another mother to feel less alone.

Our experiences shape us, and not always in the way we had hoped. But once we learn to walk through life with our grief, what we do with those life-changing experiences is ultimately up to us.

———

Discussion Questions

When the author's baby ended up in the NICU after a premature birth, she struggled to balance her new role as a mother with her established identity as a nurse practitioner in the NICU. Ultimately she reflected on how this dual identity made her both a better medical practitioner and a better mother. She also revealed the tension in her marriage, as she and her husband navigated her son's stay in the NICU, and how distance sprang up between them until they were able to be honest about their feelings and find a way to grieve together.

1. The author shared the different coping mechanisms she and her husband used during their son's NICU journey and how this caused tension in their marriage. Have you experienced

anything like this with your partner during a crisis? How did you navigate it?

2. While her son was in the NICU, and then during his initial homecoming, the author was in survival mode, stuffing feelings back down—which caused a breakdown later. How can we create space for grieving in the midst of hardship?

12

MY LUCK IS KISMET

DR. ANGELA CHAUDHARI

I have always been pretty lucky. Things usually go my way. My mother, a devout Hindu, would say this is "kismet" or my fate, pre-destined by a higher authority or possibly by my good works in a previous life. I have always called it luck.

I was born as the third and youngest child in an educated immigrant family who had moved to the United States from India to find a better life. I grew up middle-class in a white, suburban, affluent neighborhood in the Midwest with many friends, family members, and support systems around me. I underwent the usual tribulations of growing up—a childhood illness, an awkward stage with horrible hair, not winning the student council presidency, and of course, embarrassing parents as a teenager. But I made it through, just like all of you.

When I applied to college and embarked on entering the world, I was lucky enough to choose where I went, not just based on admissions but on where I was able to get a full academic scholarship. And then I gained direct admission to medical school. So six years after graduating from high school, powering through my four-year college in two years and completing four years of medical school, I was a full-fledged medical doctor. I understood the power and importance of hard work, dedication, commitment, and a loving, supportive family. I felt pretty lucky to be where I was.

My luck continued. After medical school, a young physician's life is decided by a computer algorithm called the National Match. I had decided in my fourth year of medical school to apply into the field of obstetrics and gynecology. I was attracted to the fast-paced and constantly changing nature of this work. I loved delivering babies, loved the connections I was able to make with my patients in the office, and loved surgery for its precision and ability to improve women's lives quickly and efficiently. I was fortunate to interview at many top programs around the country and to match at my top choice in St. Louis, Missouri.

Moving to St. Louis began a new chapter in my life. I started my training in obstetrics and gynecology and embarked on what most physicians consider the most harrowing part of their career. One-hundred-plus-hour work-weeks, on call in the hospital for forty hours straight on a regular basis, and sleeplessness became routine parts of life. But I had the privilege of caring for women as they prepared to become mothers, as they delivered their children, as they celebrated, and as they grieved. I hugged and cried and learned from so many women at these critical moments in their lives.

At a time when many young physicians are just barely surviving, I thrived—in an environment of constant learning and caring and feeling, despite the physical exhaustion that the work created. I came to love academic medicine, utilizing cutting-edge, evidence-based research to create the best outcomes for my patients while also fostering relationships and connection. I made lifelong friends and built a support system for myself. I also met the man who would become my husband and the father of my children.

After my husband and I completed all our medical residencies, fellowships, and certifications, we began our first "real jobs" in Salt Lake City, Utah. We were excited to find our professional niches and worked hard to set the foundation for successful careers in academic medicine. We worked, traveled, and truly enjoyed new experiences together.

As we considered growing our family, we took the obligatory pre-baby international vacation with our parents, returning to India where they were born. We enjoyed our travels—eating delicious food, marveling at new sights, reconnecting with family—and grieved at the poverty of our home country. It was a sorrowful reminder of our good luck and our parents' dedication to education, hard work, and sacrifice that had brought them to the United States and allowed us to create our current lives.

On our return to that real life, we dove back into work. We spent our days doing clinical work and our evenings preparing lectures, writing papers, and creating educational curriculum.

We were happy, feeling settled in a new home, and decided it was time to take on the next chapter in our lives together: parenthood. As a gynecologist who had counseled so many women trying to conceive, I warned my husband about the delays and difficulties that often occurred with getting pregnant. But again, our luck won out. We received a positive test within four months, and I felt well. No pain, no cramping, no morning sickness, but I was pragmatic and knew the risks: One in three pregnancies ends in miscarriage in the first three months. Prior to our first ultrasound, I braced my husband for the worst: I might still have a miscarriage, but we could always try again.

We approached the day of our first ultrasound with cautious excitement. A dear friend and colleague performed the procedure, and as she and I watched the screen, our eyes widened. I remember the clear sound of worry in my husband's voice as he watched us, not understanding the black-and-white pictures on the screen. "What is it? A miscarriage? A heartbeat? Two heads?"

My colleague and I slowly shook our heads in disbelief: "Not a miscarriage and definitely a heartbeat ... in fact two ... and two heads." We were having twins.

We were having twins. We immediately canceled the rest of our workday and sat down to lunch where we exchanged less than ten words over the next hour. I felt so many emotions when I saw the ultrasound—astonishment, disbelief, stress, but mostly fear. You see, there are different types of twins. Fraternal twins, as they are commonly known, arise from two eggs, whereas identical twins arise from the same egg. It was clear, based on that very first ultrasound, that our twins were identical. As an obstetrician/gynecologist, the fear of the complications that occur with identical twins was overwhelming. High risks of miscarriage, preterm delivery, twin-to-twin transfusion, and long-term developmental complications were coursing through my brain, and vocalizing them to my husband made them even more real.

Yet we persevered. We made it through the first trimester without complications and braced ourselves for the worst at the time of our anatomy ultrasound. The twins' development was on track, but there were some minor signs that something may be wrong. We decided to pursue an amniocentesis to ease our worry, a test that requires placing a needle into each twin's sac to remove fluid and check each fetus's chromosome makeup. The test confirmed no issues with the chromosomes, and we were having twin boys. We breathed our first sigh of relief and tried to enjoy the prospect of being parents to healthy twins.

But there was still fear. Every three to four weeks, I went to my doctor's for another growth ultrasound. And each month, I was told they were both growing—but at different rates. "Baby B slightly smaller, Baby A slightly larger, but no need for concern."

At thirty weeks, I had a bout with preterm labor that landed me in the hospital, and I was instructed to no longer work on my feet. The time off work should have been rejuvenating—time to nest, read, and prepare. Instead, I was frenetic. I couldn't sleep, couldn't eat, and couldn't focus to read. The worry about the twins' growth and the potential for early delivery consumed my thoughts.

By thirty-three weeks, the growth difference between the twins was significant, but they both seemed to still have good placental blood flow. Our doctors recommended more time for growth and development before delivery.

By thirty-six weeks, it was clear: Baby B was not growing and had stopped having appropriate blood flow from the placenta. We needed to move forward with delivery.

When we arrived on the day of delivery, my husband and I were both excited but anxious. Would both twins cry, eat, be healthy? Would they need an ICU stay? Would they be able to come home with us?

In the operating room for my cesarean section, I hit my professional stride. I was back in my element. I knew my team, my nurses, my doctors. My pragmatism won out; all would be OK because I was back in the operating room, calling for my own sutures and materials for my cesarean delivery from behind the surgical drape. My husband watched me in this mode and thought I was crazy. I had been consumed with anxiety about this delivery, but in the moment, I was strong, laughing—ready.

The moments the twins were born will be forever fresh in my memory. Immobile on the operating table under harsh white lights, I listened to my colleagues discuss my surgery from behind the drape while watching my husband stand next to me to take photos and hear their first cries. From the moment of delivery, the boys were whisked away to the infant warmer to be attended to by the pediatrics team. They were so small but had strong cries and good Apgar scores.

As they were quickly bundled up to be taken to the nursery for monitoring, I remember vividly pushing my husband away to go with them. I needed him present in the nursery because I couldn't be there at that moment. I could handle the operating room alone—it was my space—but I wanted him there with the boys in the nursery.

After surgery and recovery, my husband rejoined me in my postpartum suite, smiling from ear to ear. He had given them their first baths and taken so many photos. We pored over those photos and debated what we should name them. We laughed and cried happy tears after months of worry and fear.

By the next morning, both boys were in our room, and we took turns holding and feeding them. We were exhausted but amazed at every finger, every toe, every movement. They were here and looked healthy, and we could finally breathe without fear for their health. We felt so grateful and so lucky.

Before newborns leave the hospital, they receive a multitude of tests and shots to ensure their well-being until their first pediatrics visit. In thirty-six of the fifty states in the US, newborns receive a hearing screen—most often the otoacoustic emissions test, a noninvasive test utilizing an earphone and microphone in a baby's ear that emits sounds and measures appropriate echoes. This test is not definitive but can give reassurance that normal hearing is intact when normal echoes are measured. When no echoes are seen, a variety of factors can create the issue, but the most serious is congenital hearing loss.

The boys were tested, and Ashym, Baby A who was born almost a pound larger, passed the first time with no issues. Aryan, Baby B, didn't pass the first time, but I was given reassurance that, given his small size and the cesarean delivery, there was likely some fluid in his ears. They would repeat the test the next day and ensure that it was normal.

On our day of discharge home, the only test left was Aryan's hearing screening, and we waited until the medical assistant was available to repeat the test. By this time, I had looked up the test and understood in more detail what it was measuring and how to look at the results. It was clear to me during the testing that, again, the results were abnormal—no signs of the echoes signaling normal hearing. Despite repeated reassurances on discharge from both my medical assistant and my seasoned pediatrician that the test was not confirmatory, the fear and anxiety that had taken hold during the pregnancy began to creep back in. The joy of having two healthy babies during their first two days of life was already a distant memory.

In all aspects of my life, I have always been the person who gets things done, who takes control of situations, who is efficient and no-nonsense. I am a "doer." Pregnancy had highlighted my discomfort with a lack of control. Getting an abnormal hearing test pushed me back out of my comfort zone and into that grey area. To try to take back control, I did everything I could to manage every other aspect of my life, arguing with my mother and husband about every detail of the twins' life: diapering, feeding, sleep schedules, and when they could be held or needed to cry it out. Meanwhile, I called everyone I knew to speed up the confirmatory testing on the hearing test. I needed some answers about what the test meant and how to move forward—what to do next. I was exhausted, sleep-deprived, emotionally spent, and scared about what having a child with a disability meant for me, my family, my professional life, and my own identity. And I felt guilty that I was even worrying about my own needs at a time when my child needed me so much.

Over the next two months, we visited audiologists in three hospitals for six confirmation tests on Aryan's hearing loss. Only one to two are required, but I needed 100 percent certainty to create my game plan and take control of the situation. On all six tests, it was confirmed: Aryan had bilateral profound sensorineural hearing loss. We underwent genetic testing to look for a congenital component that might have led to other developmental delays or to his twin brother being at risk for progressive hearing loss, imaging to look for abnormalities in the growth of his ear, and heart and lung tests to look for other abnormalities from birth. Our testing returned with no other abnormalities or identifiable reason for the hearing loss. He could hear nothing when we spoke, nothing when his brother cried, nothing when we tried to comfort him.

In retrospect, it is easy to see I was having an acute grief reaction for the loss of the future that I had planned for my son, our family, myself, and my career. I thought at that time that all my luck had finally run out, and that all of that bad luck had been placed on my child. That this was somehow my fault, and I should have had more personal setbacks to save my son from his future difficulties.

At that time, I coped in the only way I knew—through control. I bought audiology textbooks and read night and day about the ear and hearing loss. I explored schools all over the country for children with hearing loss. I read about different communication methods: sign language, auditory-oral, cued speech, and total communication methods. I learned about cochlear implants by watching videos covering how these surgeries were performed by otolaryngologists and when they should be done. I read the audiology literature on how to map cochlear implants. I read about speech therapy and learned best practices to begin at home.

During this time, I went back to my work as an obstetrician-gynecologist. But the education and career that had defined me since I was eighteen years old had to come second to the needs of my family. I spoke to my boss—my chairman, a family man himself with many children—and explained the situation. Looking back, I was so lucky to have him as my boss at that time. As a mentor, he explained that life would give you challenges but that you didn't need to derail your career because of them. He explained how being part-time wouldn't change my family situation, but it would be detrimental to my academic career and progressing forward. Instead, he was able to help me create a plan where I could back off on some of my clinical and academic responsibilities, keep my position, and develop time for appointments, therapy, and potential surgery.

Aryan was fitted for hearing aids at six weeks of age, and by three months, I was already exploring cochlear implant surgery. At that time, children were not approved for surgery by insurance in the United States until after twelve months of age. I spent countless hours writing letters, speaking on the phone, and drumming up support at a state level for coverage of services for surgery

In the meantime, I continued strict schedules for the twins, which drove my husband, mother, and nanny crazy. My need for control of my situation was paramount.

Finally, when Aryan was eleven months of age, our insurance approvals came through, and surgery was scheduled. We rejoiced over the small win, but my anxiety again won out. I rushed to retest both of my twins for hearing loss for the umpteenth time. Cochlear implant surgery was permanent and destroyed any residual hearing a child has. What if I had the wrong twin diagnosed? I needed to confirm one more time before we could proceed, despite numerous reassurances from our audiologist that there was no mistake.

Finally, we were ready. We traveled for the surgery to Chicago, to a world-class pediatric cochlear implant center. We had decided to pursue bilateral implant surgery to avoid the need to come back for a second procedure.

Back in the hospital, sitting with Aryan before his surgery, most parents would be so worried about sending their young child in to surgery. But I was relieved, excited, ready. Finally, I had some sense of control over what happened to my child. I sat with my husband and two dearest friends for over seven hours that day, waiting for a call from our surgeon. We finally received the call that all had gone well. It had been technically difficult based on his small size, but they expected both implants to be a success.

After the first night, the rest of recovery went smoothly. Aryan was quick to crawl around and eat and was always ready to play with his brother. We were finally able to breathe a sigh of relief. All we had worked for over the last year had been successful. Our luck felt like it was back on.

He still was unable to hear us though. After cochlear implant surgery, activation of the implant—or "turning it on" —happens about four to six weeks after surgery, and we couldn't wait! We had watched so many videos of children at the time of their activation with looks of surprise on their faces and giggles or cries that ensued after hearing sound for the first time. We prepared ourselves and our families, with both sets of grandparents eagerly standing by to receive the text with the video of his activation. I remember so clearly holding Aryan as he slept in my arms that morning in the audiologist's office, with my heart fluttering in excitement over what he would first hear.

But what happened didn't match the videos. Aryan's activation occurred while peacefully sleeping in our arms. Despite playing loud music and talking loudly, Aryan wouldn't wake up. He slept through the entire activation. My husband and I wept. We were certain that with no responses to the noise, he still couldn't hear us. Our audiologist reassured us again and again: Every activation is different, every child responds differently; give us time to do the mappings. Again, our ability to control responses, to control outcomes, to control ... was out of our control.

Over the next four years, we had more audiology visits and second opinions than we could count—in more than ten locations in three states. Everyone agreed: The tests said Aryan could hear, but he wasn't hearing the same as other kids with bilateral cochlear implants. By this time, we had changed jobs and moved across the country to access better speech therapy and an auditory-oral education for Aryan in a large urban center.

Aryan was always trying to talk, but his speech was garbled and difficult to understand. He became frustrated when others couldn't understand him and threw tantrums due to that frustration. Even with these frustrations, his teachers recognized his intelligence. He was voraciously reading books at the age of four and trying to use them to communicate, pointing at things and trying to form the words to tell us what he was thinking. He was responding to directions via lip reading, though he couldn't hear what his teachers were asking.

We were encouraged to seek out yet another opinion in another state or be faced with the reality that Aryan should change his mode of communication from spoken language to American Sign Language in a new school. He was so intelligent, but speaking might not be the mode in which he could communicate.

We were heartbroken. The implants were not working the way they should, and his inability to hear would keep him out of the hearing world that his family lived in. We grieved, as everything felt like loss: his inability to hear us as his parents, his future education prospects, our inability to communicate with him until we learned sign language. Was his kismet to never hear us or communicate with us in spoken language?

That recommendation to seek out yet another opinion changed the course of Aryan's life at age five. We spent eight hours in our first audiology appointment at the new center, with a full team of skilled audiologists and speech pathologists. They were baffled at why all the electronic responses were present and correct but he didn't seem to hear in the expected way. They decided to extend his appointment and spent the entire day "starting from scratch," as though he had just been newly implanted and activated for the first time that day. Aryan was engaged throughout the day—coloring, responding to directions via lipreading, turning to new noises, and as the day progressed, looking at us in surprise and saying "yes," he could hear something new and different. He could hear our voices.

The rest of this story is not about luck. It is about a child who works so hard every single day to learn to listen and speak in a hearing world with cochlear implants. Within two weeks of that audiology appointment, Aryan's speech was already becoming more recognizable. His education began to move forward at record speed as he learned new vocabulary, which he had already known from his reading but was now learning to articulate in speech.

As the weeks progressed to years, Aryan graduated from his auditory-oral school and mainstreamed into a prestigious private school, joining his twin brother. He has excelled in all aspects of his academic work as a straight-A student, has amazing friends, and is active in so many extracurriculars— varsity golf, water polo, and Model United Nations. He is an active participant in his classes and actively looks for opportunities to speak and present to groups. He has learned to advocate for himself and what he needs to be successful socially and academically.

I am the luckiest person. I am fortunate to be surrounded by family and friends. I have a profession that gives me meaning and joy every day and allows me to provide for our family. My husband and I have the privilege of three healthy children who are curious, respectful, empathetic, and caring about the people and world around them. And I get to watch Aryan thrive in all his communities through sheer work ethic.

So maybe my mother was right: My kismet allows me to share this wonderful life with people I care about. And I think Aryan's kismet is absolutely to change the world for the better.

Discussion Questions

The author talks about her difficult choice when going back to work over how to balance career ambitions with caring for a child with a disability—and how she was fortunate to have a supportive boss and mentor who helped her find a middle ground so she could move forward in both aspects of life. She also talks about the role luck has played, and how when her son was born with hearing loss, she felt like it was punishment for having been lucky most of her life up until then.

1. While most parents experience some degree of tension between work and home responsibilities, it's often heightened for parents of children with disabilities. Have you ever felt like you had to choose between succeeding at work or at home? How did you navigate this? What kind of support did you seek out (or wish you'd sought out)?

2. What role do you believe luck plays in our lives? Have you ever felt like you were being punished for previous good fortune, or like you were waiting for the other shoe to drop? Why do you think we are sometimes unable to trust and enjoy the good things that happen to us?

13

POSTPARTUM UNFILTERED

CAMILLE SEIGLE

L ast week, someone asked me, "Did you always want to be a mother?"

My initial response was yes, followed by a long pause to truly ponder the question. *Actually, I don't remember*, I thought to myself. There I was, playing with my fifteen-month-old daughter on the floor of her bedroom and really thinking about this question for the first time. Because while I always had ideas and thoughts of what it meant to be a mother or what type of mother I would be, I had never really thought about if I *wanted* to be a mom.

For me, after having my first child, I had no idea who I was, what I had become, or what I wanted to be. There are so many things I wish I'd known were OK to feel. So here, I want to share my real postpartum experience. I want to get honest in the hope that it helps you know you're not alone, and that what you feel is OK. I want to talk about the reality of having a baby that's often covered up with Instagram filters and posed pictures two weeks postpartum, which show women looking amazing and feeling great. (If this is you, congratulations, as you won the genetics and postpartum lottery.)

But that's not my story. So let me take you on my journey.

Following the Rules

From an early age, I followed rules and did what I was told. I was taught how to behave, how to ask questions, and how to have a perspective. I learned the difference between right and wrong—or at least what my parents viewed as right and wrong. I now recognize how this shaped my thoughts of how I wanted to raise a family and what it meant to me.

Back then, I wanted to have the "perfect" family. It took me a long time to acknowledge that there is no perfect. We are all learning and growing throughout this experience we call life.

Though I didn't fully know what perfect was or who defined it for us, I had the idea that this equated to growing up in a life of privilege. I don't know where this vision came from. My parents got divorced when I was young, and while my mom did stay at home during our younger years, she also worked at points during our childhood. Also, weirdly, in my vision of motherhood, my kids were always toddlers and never babies. I had no context for what women went through post-childbirth.

As it turns out, I was in for a rude awakening.

Expectations

Why on earth does no one tell you what to expect once you have a baby? Sure, there are books with advice on taking care of your body postpartum, bonding with your baby, and breast-feeding. Oh, and my personal favorite piece of advice: Nap when your baby is napping. But really what this amounts to is *good luck*.

Why isn't anyone painting the real picture of what you need to expect and helping women prepare for these changes? For example, if you're in a relationship, get ready to have fights with your partner about absolutely nothing. Get ready to react to everyone and everything, because your hormones are slapping you in the face. If you're a working mom, get ready to question your career and experience mom-guilt for most of the choices you make. Also, get ready for no one to ask how you are doing, because they're so focused on the baby. And if you were like me, you weren't sleeping, you were thirsty and hungry from breastfeeding, you had hemorrhoids and weren't able to poop, and you were losing a lot of hair when you showered (if you even could shower).

Oh, and maybe, like me, you were also questioning whether you wanted to be a mom.

The Day It All Changed

In January 2020, I delivered a healthy, beautiful baby girl. And while I'm not the most emotional person (as friends and family can attest), I remember looking at my husband as I gave birth and shedding tears. Watching your body work so hard to deliver something so magnificent is incredible. The gift of life.

The first night in the hospital was surreal. I was tired and in pain, and I was a mother who had just given birth to my first child—someone I was not at all prepared to take care of. The anxiety that came up made me want to throw up. I took a deep breath and swallowed. Up until this point in my life, I hadn't needed to take care of anything else of this magnitude. Just last week, someone had told me how similar having a puppy is to having a baby. *You have no idea*, I thought now.

Bringing a human into this world made me question so much about myself, my husband, our family, and the choices we were going to make. I had this sudden flash in my head of all the unknowns sitting in front of me. Choices that ranged from what she should wear today to how we would raise a daughter who valued kindness and giving back in a world that feels complex.

As someone who values control, having a baby tests those

limits every day. This is one of my biggest life lessons. I offer to any new mom that if you can *really live in the moment*, you will find more happiness.

If only I had taken my own advice.

At the hospital, I was caught up in the logistics of completing everything on my checklist. *Did I read all the material, and did I complete all the paperwork to leave the hospital?* While my husband was right there in the hospital and offering to help, I also didn't know what I needed or how to delegate. There were obvious things he couldn't help with such as breastfeeding, however there are about twenty thousand other things that our partners can help with if we ask.

For me, asking is the hardest part. As a woman who has been able to *do it herself*, I kept saying I did *not* need help. But asking for help is powerful. It doesn't mean you're weak; it means you're strong enough to see that you need others to make you better. *You do not need to do it all yourself.* There is a lot of help around you that is willing and able. (Insert LOL if you had a baby in the year 2020.)

Work Will Always Be There

When I had my daughter, I was working full-time, and I found that learning how to manage a career and a family added another layer of battling limiting beliefs and constant reframing to get the balancing act right. On the second day in the hospital after having the baby, I reached out to my boss, checked my email, and contacted benefits. If you're reading this and thinking you did the same thing, well, that says a lot about the state of American work standards and what working women think is normal and OK.

I chose before maternity leave to check in with my boss on a monthly basis, as I wanted to ensure I wasn't fully disconnected. Looking back, I did it partly out of fear over what I might miss out on and partly as a reminder that I still existed.

While my boss had encouraged me to disconnect, I did not and could not. I gave up so much control when I had a child, and work was something I felt like I could control. It was also a part of my life I felt good at, and with all the uncertainty a new baby would bring, I needed a reminder that I was capable and competent in something.

I've spoken to so many women who also stay connected to work on their maternity leave. Many share the sentiment of being bored along with the fear of missing opportunities if they disconnect. As I reflect on my time, though, I'm so mad at myself for *not* disconnecting and instead putting my time into something else—into really thinking about what my values were and what I needed to do for myself. Even now, I struggle with my identity outside of work, and I've talked to many other women who share this feeling. So if you're fortunate enough to be given maternity leave, do yourself a favor: Do not check your email. Disconnect. If you're in this position, trust that work will always be there.

Moving Through the Fog

The first six weeks felt like a constant repeat of the American movie, *Groundhog Day*. Eat, sleep, and poop were on repeat for the baby. I don't remember much, which I think is partly due to my selective memory shielding me from the mental and physical pain I felt. As I look back on texts from the first few weeks, many asked how our daughter was doing. Others asked how breastfeeding was going. Very few asked how *I* was doing.

My standard responses to friends were, "People are coming over, which is great and annoying," or "Vagina is killing me, and otherwise I'm great." While that's what I was sharing to friends, I look at my journal from the first week and see a very different reflection—one that I don't remember writing, but as I read it back, I resonate with each emotion it shows.

I am tired. I feel alone. I don't know what I am doing. Everyone is giving me advice, and I don't even know what I want to do. How do people do this? Mentally, I am so tired. I don't want to go back to work. Why am I even thinking about work? But really, I can barely go to the bathroom without screaming in pain. It burns to pee from my stitches, and I need to pat myself dry after the burn. I cannot poop, yet I feel like a cow. I don't even look like myself. I look in the mirror and barely see the woman I was before. How can you love someone so much and be so sad about everything? When does this get easier? How do I ask for help? I have help, but then I feel guilty as I should be able to do it myself. My boobs hurt.

I remember my journal entry that day ended abruptly, as I looked down on my bed and saw blood. Lots of blood. I hobbled as fast as I could to the bathroom to see a clot about the size of a golf ball exit my body. My doctor had told me to expect blood clots and that I didn't need to worry about anything golf ball size or less. Anxiety set in again. *Well, it is the size of a golf ball. So do I call—or not?*

I called my husband in to look.

Note: If you are in the type of relationship in which you do not poop or fart around your partner, I would really consider letting your guard down prior to childbirth. Your partner will love you more, and you will need them in critical moments like this.

Given that my husband is a golfer, he argued that the clot was slightly smaller than a golf ball. While I smiled for a second, after he changed the sheets, I cried on the floor for the next hour—feeling overwhelmed.

Find Your Support Network

My watch buzzed to remind me it was time to pump and breastfeed. While many women loved this experience and the bonding it created, I did not. I'm not sure which I disliked more: pumping, breastfeeding, or the guilt I felt for disliking it.

Breastfeeding, while easier, created an uncertainty every time my daughter ate. I didn't know how much milk she was getting and felt like I was performing the mile in gym class—timing myself to complete the task. And while the boob allowed for easy access, the pain was not worth it.

The pump, on the other hand, made me feel like a cow getting milked. The thought of the noise the pump makes as it sucks out your milk still makes me want to vomit.

I'd never had a time in my life when I worked so hard for something and then I questioned it all. I had zero confidence about what I was doing as a new mom. I felt like a private investigator trying to understand every rash my daughter had on her face and why her poop looked a certain way. I wrote notes to myself about questions to ask the doctor or look up online. And while my doctor had advised me to avoid Google, I didn't listen. This added anxiety and emotional twists in my hormones when every search result pointed to an ungodly disease. I found myself not sleeping at night and instead looking at message boards to determine what to do.

After the endless Google searches, I would then find myself texting a few close friends to ask what I should do. What did they think it is? One of the funniest replies I received was from a friend who told me that if I saw anything odd on the baby's face or body, to just put some breast milk on it, as it would cure everything. And somehow, it did.

During this time, I needed friends who would tell it like it was and share what worked for them and how to get through the early days. Most importantly, I needed nonjudgmental friends who would share what worked for them while recognizing it might not work for me.

If you have friends who tell you to change the way you're doing something or judge you for your choices, might I suggest that you find new ones. Life is too short, and as a new mom, there is enough pressure on you without anyone else judging your decisions.

Asking for Help

By my six-week appointment, the pandemic had hit and the world had changed dramatically. It still hurt to walk, and I was not healed. This was my first visit outside of the house by myself, though, so I was energized yet nervous.

When I got to the doctor's office, I sat down with the standard questionnaire to analyze if I had postpartum depression and anxiety. I didn't need a form to tell me I was depressed and anxious. I didn't want to do anything except sleep. I felt no joy despite having a new baby, and I had no idea who I was. But even with awareness of all that, I also knew how to fill out the questionnaire and go on my way without being questioned by my doctor.

At my appointment, the doctor said my stitches were not healing well and she might need to restitch me if they continued to heal that way.

"How are you doing?" she asked, changing the course of the appointment away from the tactical issues into the harder to quantify—and seemingly harder to resolve—emotional realm.

I paused before deciding to answer her question as thoroughly as I could. I was feeling everything: Grateful to have a new baby, yet upset that almost no one was asking how I was. Relieved to have help during the night so I could sleep, yet no matter how much help I had, I still felt tired. Lucky to have a loving husband by my side, yet I had no desire to be touched or even looked at. Thankful that my body could give birth to another human, yet weaker and more fragile than ever before.

How can I be experiencing all these emotions at once? I wondered after hearing myself speak.

After my monologue ended, my doctor spoke. "What do you think about increasing your anxiety medication?"

I was in such paralysis that I didn't know what I should do or what might help. I just felt numb. "I don't really feel like I'm in a position to be able to make a choice," I answered.

She suggested I think about it, and also that I find a new therapist who specialized in postpartum care.

I left the appointment acutely aware of how exhausted and overwhelmed I was. *How am I supposed to find time for a therapist?* I wondered.

A few weeks passed with no change in my energy or emotions. My husband began comparing me to Eeyore from *Winnie the Pooh*—and I agreed.

On one particular day in early April, my emotions were at an all-time high. I walked downstairs and began feeding my daughter, and I felt like my whole body was itching. I wanted to jump out of my skin. As I breastfed, I looked down at my stomach and felt a wave of shame and guilt—shame that my body looked the way it did, and guilt for even thinking such a thought. I couldn't calm these racing thoughts. I tried taking a deep breath and struggled to exhale.

At the same moment, my dog tapped me to be let out. I handed my baby to my husband, walked back up the stairs, opened the door to the deck, and then looked down at the ground.

What would happen if I jumped? I wondered. *Would I live or would I die?* Tears rolled down from my eyes. I knew people loved me, yet I was incapable of loving myself. I had everything, yet I was not able to see that in this moment. I had never had a thought like this before and was shocked at the intensity in which it arrived. I felt so alone.

If only I'd known then how many women would eventually tell me they had struggled with similar terrifying thoughts.

My dog then tapped me to go back inside. I was still so numb yet followed her back indoors as my thoughts swirled.

Once inside, I heard my daughter cry. In the previous weeks, her cry had brought me frustration and uncertainty, yet this time, it was different. I felt hope. It was as if her cry was everyone who loved me, speaking to me and telling me to *have hope and believe.*

I walked downstairs with tears streaming down my face, and at that moment, I identified myself as a mother for the first time. I took my daughter from my husband's arms and held her close. My tears continued as hers stopped. She needed me.

I had been crying a lot in the early days, as my hormones were so dysregulated, so my husband didn't think twice about my reaction. Yet for me, it was a moment I will never forget.

Many women are not given a guide on how to be a mother or how to understand the emotions and feelings they're about to experience. As a mother in the early weeks after your baby's birth, you'll likely go through hell and back as you try to take care of something that's giving you nothing in return. For me, this moment of a paused cry was enough to spark a feeling of worth in myself. It also was enough to make me recognize I needed help—even if I didn't yet know exactly how to get it.

The Light in the Darkness

Later that afternoon, I went on a walk with my daughter to the park a few blocks from my house—a place I had frequented with my mother-in-law prior to her death. We would often sit on a specific bench, watch people walk by, and talk. She passed away quite suddenly when I was three months pregnant. The last conversation we had was a FaceTime call with my husband and me when we shared that we were having a baby girl.

As I sat down on the bench, I felt her presence with me. I felt her say everything was going to be OK. I felt a sense of hope. It's hard to explain what hope feels like when it enters your body, but for me, it felt like an energy that allowed for a sense of calm. It allowed for a moment of pause and a memory of feeling capable.

I walked back home with this sense of hope and a question that I still ask myself daily: *Who do I want to be, and how do I want to show up for myself?*

While this day was amazing, it wasn't followed only by other amazing days. Instead, it was followed by more hardship and a deeper recognition that I needed help. So I found a therapist who specialized in postpartum care, and I began working with her regularly. This allowed me to get comfortable with being uncomfortable.

It also stretched my understanding of how I needed to be kind to myself. This meant asking for help from my family and, most importantly, my husband.

Before, whenever my husband would offer to do something for me, I always said no. But now I started to say yes, even just once per day, and built in activities that made me feel more human—like going on a walk by myself, working out for twenty minutes, even taking a bath. As a new mom, I needed to start saying yes to myself.

Returning to Work

I went back to work during the pandemic. My daughter was just over four months old, and I decided I was officially done breastfeeding and would slowly stop pumping. Some of the advice other working moms gave me around returning to work was as follows:

- Come back in the middle of the week so your return is easier.
- Set up the breaks in your day for pumping/feeding early on to ensure your team knows you need this.

- Create boundaries around your working hours.
- Prioritize.

All of these were helpful, yet there were a lot of situations for which I wasn't prepared. For example, during one of my first weeks back, a male coworker asked me, "How was your vacation?" I paused and took a few deep breaths. He had no idea what I'd just gone through; his perception was that I'd been on a mushroom-foraging journey to find myself in the rainforest of Peru. At that moment, I was so frustrated and felt so alone. I wish I could say that this was the only situation like this I encountered. I share this, as it's important to recognize that many women go back to work when they're still recovering emotionally and mentally, and yet they're expected to show up and perform as normal.

Looking back, I wish I'd taken more time off. My employer provided a long maternity leave, yet it didn't feel long enough. I felt like my daughter was just starting to interact and engage when it was time to go back to work. Working from home brought the additional complexity of hearing her cry or laugh while I was in meetings and unable to go be with her. But it also meant I could get in a wave or kiss during a five-minute break. These experiences brought on different emotions for me. Somedays I felt so grateful I was nearby to see her, and other days I felt so guilty that I was nearby yet in meetings all day. Each day, I would go back to the questions of: *Who do I want to be? And how do I want to show up for myself?*

Moving Forward

I still think it is funny that the first time I remember anyone asking me if I wanted to be a mother was once my baby was born. The hardships of my postpartum experience leave me questioning whether I'll ever have a second child. While I was fortunate to get pregnant easily and have a healthy pregnancy and baby, I'm not sure I can emotionally manage another postpartum experience.

It's critical to discuss the hardships of postpartum, and I believe we must normalize what each woman experiences. We need to share our stories, support each other, and understand the truth of how a new parent is *really* feeling. We need to recognize that women and men might be struggling with their own identity, suffering from intense levels of anxiety and depression, and finding it almost impossible to see through the clouds of despair.

You're not alone in this journey. I think the more people we share these truths with, the better we can prepare ourselves, our partners, and our families for the road ahead. Motherhood encompasses so many emotions at once, and each age and stage our kids pass through offers us distinct challenges and endless opportunities for growth. I am so grateful for my daughter, as she has turned out to be my biggest teacher.

If I've learned one thing these past five years, it's this: When we know that we are not alone, it's a little easier to hold onto hope. And hope, as it turns out, carries us through the darkest times and reminds us that light will eventually shine through.

Discussion Questions

The author writes about struggling with her identity and feelings about being a mother after giving birth. She eventually seeks help for postpartum depression and learns to seek help in all aspects of her life, including sharing her story to normalize the hardship of the postpartum experience.

1. The author talks about how mothers on social media often filter out the hard parts of postpartum life in favor of the perfect Instagrammable moments. What do you think is behind our urge to make things look easier than they are?
2. The author talks about her inability to ask for help. Why do you think women, specifically, are often so reluctant to ask for and accept help? How can we show up for each other differently during the postpartum period? How can we give ourselves greater permission to seek out and accept help?

14

THE ROLLER COASTER OF HOPE

DR. JAIME KNOPMAN

From the age of eight, I knew I wanted to be a doctor. In the second grade, I read a book about Elizabeth Blackwell, the first woman in the US to receive a medical degree, and I had an Oprah-like aha moment: *I'm going to be a doctor!* And while my vision of what kind of medicine I'd practice would change frequently, my passion for helping others never diminished.

I was a premed student at U. Penn, and shortly after graduating, I went on to medical school at Mount Sinai where my passion for women's health, specifically fertility medicine, was solidified. As a fertility doctor, I've found that three words seem to dominate the conversations I have with my patients: *hope, roller coaster,* and *journey.*

Thinking back on my career, including my time counseling women and the intimate moments I have been privileged to be a part of, I am overcome with emotion. My memory is flooded with images of the individuals with whom I have partnered on their journey to parenthood. Some are smiling and some are crying. Some are giddy and some are despondent. I often remember where I was when I gave them the news: *You are pregnant. You are having twins.* Opening emails of baby pictures. Watching little ones grow up in Christmas cards.

The negatives are equally etched in my memories: *I no longer see a heartbeat. The transfer was not successful. There are no viable embryos. I don't recommend another round of IVF. It's time to consider an alternative way to achieve parenthood.* Each of these conversations and relationships shaped my path, not only as a physician but also as a mother, a wife, a daughter, and a friend. I firmly believe that we are a conglomeration of our past. And I am a conglomeration of the experiences I have shared with my patients. Their journeys have shaped mine, including how I've cared for and guided those who came after them.

Medicine is so much more than what we learn in school, from textbooks, or in residency. Being a good doctor is not about knowing the most information. While our clinical expertise is important, the true essence of what makes a good physician is how we marry this knowledge with empathy. We must possess these attributes in order to best serve our patients as they wrestle with difficult decisions.

What I hope patients take away from this book is that fertility treatment is a journey. Unfortunately for most of us, it is not a linear path. That dream of drinking a bit too much red wine, having sex, and two weeks later seeing a smiley face or a plus sign on a stick doesn't always come true. In fact, it rarely does. For many, making peace with a modification or monumental change in plans is what allows people to reach their ultimate goal: parenthood.

The most important ingredient in achieving a family is resilience. Falling and failing is going to happen. It's inevitable. But the ability to gather yourself together, to mourn the losses, and to push forward up the hill will almost certainly translate into parenthood. And although the result might not mirror the image you had when playing house as a child, it will be your reality. It will be your family.

When I started my career, I didn't really understand how complex the doctor-patient relationship is. I saw medicine as black and white. You have low egg quantity—you do IVF. Your uterus is damaged—you find a surrogate. You are lacking sperm—you find a sperm donor. But for most women, it is not that simple. Decisions are wrought with emotions, long-held beliefs, and childhood dreams. Telling a woman who always wanted to birth and breastfeed a child that she can't is not simple. She must mourn this loss, and it's up to me to help her find a way to move forward.

I am fascinated by grief—how we process it, how we deal with it, and how we move through it, particularly when faced with uncontrollable situations. While Elisabeth Kübler-Ross and her Five Stages of Grief were briefly addressed in medical school, I only recently realized that the process is not fluid. Just because there are five stages of grief does not mean individuals spend an equal amount of time in each stage. In fact, many people linger in one stage, struggling to move forward. The *rut factor*, as I call it, can hinder one's ability to take the next step. Some people are overcome by anger and isolate from everyone around them. Some are drowning in denial and won't listen to anyone, including their medical team. Some are so wrought with depression that they cannot imagine a future.

After a divorce and a cancer diagnosis, I was able to empathize with my patients in a way I never had before. I did not suffer from infertility and, given my line of work, have always felt somewhat guilty for easily becoming pregnant. But I, too, have suffered from loss, grief, and confusion. Like my patients, I have also questioned: *Why me? What if?* and *Now what?* I have sat on my bed, listening to sad music while nursing a glass of rosé. I have resisted getting out of my PJs, chafed at celebrating someone else's joy when I felt nothing but sadness, and smiled while holding back tears. But in those moments, with the help of others, I found the courage to get back up and keep fighting.

For any couple or individual going through infertility, negative pregnancy tests and day one of the menstrual cycle can be terrible. The anticipation and possibility of your dream comes crashing down, not to mention how awful the plummeting of your hormones and pain from cramps can be. I have found that this day is best spent mourning what could have been. Feeling the pain from the loss of possibility is healthy. It hurts, but loss is not supposed to be easy. Allow yourself the space to be sad. Don't ignore the grief you feel. As a physician, I try to provide patients with space on these darkest of days. Although I believe making future plans and designing upcoming treatment strategies is essential in maintaining hope, timing is important. For most of us who receive bad news, processing it and talking about what to do next is not something we can digest in the span of a five-minute phone call. We need time—time to process the loss and regain strength to look toward the future.

This insight, combined with becoming a patient myself after my cancer diagnosis, helped me modify the way I deliver bad news. As a young physician, I used to give bad news quickly. I would call the patient; talk fast, using medical terms; and then cross it off my list. Like most doctors, I was uncomfortable with the negative—with the unexpected outcome and what I saw as my failure. I couldn't sit in that discomfort with my patients. But personal growth has led me to change my professional demeanor. I now speak slowly—well, as slow as a girl born and bred in New York City can—pause frequently, and ask my patients if and when they will be ready to review their results. I sit in my discomfort, because I believe it allows them time to process their emotions, gather their thoughts, and consider their options.

Parenthood is accessible for everyone if we are willing to accept every potential path to this destination. IUI, IVF, donor gametes, gestational carriers, adoption—these treatments all represent avenues to becoming a parent. However, it is through letting go of our commitment to a specific route that we may find the best path to our final destination.

A friend and I recently took our daughters and their friends to an amusement park. As we pulled into the parking lot, I looked out and knew my stomach was doomed. This was going to be a rough day for someone who gets carsick. The ten-year-olds, on the other hand, were squealing with delight. The more twists and turns the ride had, the more excited they became. They lacked fear or any of the various maladies we acquire as we age that make flying through the air upside down unappealing.

I grabbed my friend's hand, screamed at the top of my lungs, and closed my eyes. I held on for dear life as we flipped forwards and backwards. I tried to brace myself for the sharp rights and lefts. In order to survive, I had to let go. I had to relinquish control. I had to believe that, as the operator promised, the ride would come to an end in exactly ninety-three seconds. I had to take the ride as it came, to breathe through the drops and await the ups.

Like many American families, we got a puppy during the pandemic. We debated what to name him and ultimately settled on Brady, after the television show *The Brady Bunch*. He is, after all, the dog of a large, blended family. And while his first name bears homage to the family in which he is being raised, his middle name, Hope, represents our family's future. Without hope, we can't move forward. We can't appreciate our present, and we certainly can't imagine a future.

The best advice I can give a patient is the same advice that has been given to me, the same advice I give to friends who are struggling and to my daughters as they navigate challenging situations: You have to know when to let go and when to hang on—even when you want to throw up or jump off or not take the next turn. Hold tight to the person next to you, behind you, and in front of you. Scream if you have to, but don't give up hope. Never stop dreaming, never stop believing, never lose the will to fight. And while this does not mean spending your life's savings to pursue fertility treatments that carry single-digit success rates, it does mean maintaining the notion of possibility.

Life isn't easy, and we all get knocked down—some in harder ways, and some many more times than others. But whether your path is marred by infertility, cancer, divorce, or death, maintaining hope will give you the strength to stand back up. You will be stronger, you will be wiser, and you will likely be a better person.

———

Discussion Questions

The author's experience as a fertility doctor has given her a front-row seat to the ups and downs of individual fertility journeys and the importance of hope along the way. She also experienced her own hardships with a divorce and a cancer diagnosis, and she writes about how letting go of control has helped her to take life as it comes and keep her own sense of hope alive.

1. The author writes about maintaining the notion of possibility while also being realistic—for example, not spending your life savings on pursuing fertility treatments that carry single-digit success rates. How do you balance these two often-opposing ideas in your own life?

2. In some cases, toxic positivity (the practice of rejecting all difficult emotions in favor of a cheerful and often falsely positive façade) can replace hope. How do we tell the difference between remaining optimistic and taking positivity to an unhealthy extreme?

CONCLUSION

As you reach the end of *Maternal Hope*, our hope is that you feel a little less alone. The stories you've read—including those of loss, resilience, and a redefinition of parenthood—were written to remind you that your struggles, your questions, and your emotions are valid. They are shared by many, even if those voices are often unheard or unseen. We hope these pages have offered you comfort and solidarity.

The journey to and through parenthood, as these essays have shown, is rarely a straight or simple path. Moving forward, we encourage you to take what you've felt—that sense of connection—and nurture it. In the process, we hope you will transition from feeling a little less alone to truly *being* less alone. Here are some actionable ways to do that:

Share Your Story

Sharing your story can be an act of healing. It might feel daunting, but opening up to a friend, joining a support group, or writing down your experiences can help you process your emotions and connect with others who understand.

Seek Out Community

Look for groups that align with your experiences. Whether it's a local meetup for parents navigating similar challenges, an online forum, or a therapeutic circle, finding your people can be transformative.

Lean on Resources

In times of hardship, resources can be lifelines. Turn to professionals, such as therapists or counselors specializing in maternal health, or explore local organizations and nonprofits that provide support. If you're unsure where to start, the resources section of this book includes suggestions that our authors have found particularly helpful for various aspects of the parenthood journey—from loss and infertility to postpartum support and child-free living.

Take Small Steps Toward Connection

Sometimes, connection starts small. A conversation with a neighbor, a coffee date with a friend, or a moment of kindness extended to another can lay the foundation for deeper relationships. As many of our contributing authors have discovered, small acts of reaching out often lead to unexpected but meaningful bonds.

Before we part, we want to offer this: The stories in this book, including ours, are proof that even in the darkest times, hope persists. Healing is not linear, and it might look different than you imagined. But with time, support, and self-compassion, you *will* find your way.

You have already taken an incredible step by picking up this book and immersing yourself in these narratives. That act of seeking connection and understanding is one of courage. As you close these pages, carry with you the knowledge that you are not alone. The world is full of others walking parallel paths, ready to support you, listen to you, and stand with you. May you move forward with renewed hope and the confidence that, whatever your journey looks like, you are not walking it alone.

ACKNOWLEDGMENTS

From Both of Us

When we first met in the workplace back in 2015, we had no idea we'd one day be writing a book, together, on a topic so personal to each of us.

From the very beginning, this project has been a labor of love, trust, and deep collaboration. We are profoundly grateful to every person who helped shape this book into what it is today.

To Whitney Bischoff Angel: Your words bring grounding and depth to the foreword. We're so honored to have your voice open this book.

To our fellow writers and contributing authors, Dr. Carli Blau, Dr. Angela Chaudhari, Melissa Connelly, Trafford Judd, Sarah Kamp, Dr. Jaime Knopman, Erin Koelliker, Christine Nguyen, Nicole Nuberg, Dr. Sonal Patel, Juana Pfadt, and Monica Royer: This work would not exist without your stories, your honesty, and your courage. You are the heartbeat of this book, and we are endlessly honored to have your voices fill these pages.

To our incredible endorsers, Dr. Simone Ahuja, Molly West Duffy, Dr. Bec Holmes, Amanda Kloots, Zibby Owens, Eve Rodsky, Dr. Neel Shah, Dr. Jessica Shepherd, Mary Catherine Starr, Andrea Syrtash, Caitlin Weaver, Jordan Younger, and Dr. Jessica Zucker: Thank you for supporting this book and helping us bring our message of hope and community to those struggling as we once did. Your encouragement helped us feel seen and validated at every stage.

To Jenny Lisk: Thank you for being our lighthouse. Your steady guidance, industry wisdom, and unwavering support made every step feel possible.

To Jocelyn Carbonara: Thank you for seeing the heart of this project and polishing every word with care and precision. Your dedication went far beyond the red pen.

To Rachel Bertsche: Your belief in us during the uncertainty of COVID gave us the confidence to begin. You held space for this idea before it ever became tangible, and we're deeply thankful.

To Caitlin Weaver: Thank you for helping us set the foundation of this work. Your insights and thoughtful feedback helped us shape the earliest versions of this book.

To George Stevens: Thank you for seeing our vision and creating a beautiful cover that showcases our purpose.

This book is not just a finished product—it's a collective story, woven together with the generosity of so many. We are deeply grateful to you all.

With love,
Ali and Camille

From Camille Seigle

I have so much gratitude for the many people who have supported, encouraged, and listened to me. You helped make this book possible. I believe the people in my life have been placed there for a reason, and I've learned something meaningful from each of you.

Ali, I want to thank you first. From the moment we met at LinkedIn, I knew we'd have a strong friendship, but I never imagined we would create something with such profound impact. I'm endlessly grateful for your ability to listen, for showing up fully as yourself, and for being the yin to my yang. We've done something incredible together here, and I'll never forget it.

To my amazing LinkedIn colleagues, many of whom have turned into my closest friends: My time with you was the most transformational seven years of my life. During that time, I changed roles multiple times, got married, had my daughter, and met Ali. I had the privilege of working with incredible leaders who helped me recognize my strengths. Thank you to my AE LSS Team, my LLS Team, my Sales Readiness Team, and my Chicago Office and Chicago Families. Each of you impacted me in powerful ways. To the thousands of people I trained, thank you for allowing me to learn from *you*. You reminded me that we all carry stories, and every one of them matters. To my closest guy friends, the ones I met at LinkedIn: Who knew we would form the relationships that we did, and that our group chat would still be going strong after all this time? You keep me grounded, make me laugh, and always believe in me. Thank you.

To my teams at Starwood and Langham: When I first started my career, I spent time in the hospitality industry and quickly learned that teamwork is the only way to get anything done. We worked long hours and created some truly magical moments. More than anything, we had *fun*. I spent way too much time in the pastry kitchen and now have a friend for life. I even gained a best friend from those years— someone who had her own journey, and who was generous enough to share it in this book. Thank you for sharing your story and for believing in me.

To my closest friends and family: Thank you for believing in me and offering the gift of friendship. I believe friends make life better, and I feel so lucky to have you in mine.

Special thanks to:

- The friend who remembers all the important dates, believes in me when I forget to believe in myself, and pushes me to dream bigger.
- My friends who live across the country in Coconut Grove, Laguna, and Pittsburgh. While it may be harder to connect these days, when we do, it feels like no time has passed.
- One of my oldest friends, whose friendship started long ago in high school. Though you spend half the year in Croatia, you still manage to text me to check in. Thank you for always being so positive and loving.
- The friend I met at LinkedIn who finally lives close by, so we can do life together with our girls. Workouts and walks with you are always a highlight of my week. Thank you for keeping it real and telling me not to go back to corporate.
- My best friend, who is doing her own incredible work in Chicago and still manages to be present for me. Thank you for reading my chapter early on, helping me make decisions, and always believing in me.
- The friend who is the most social person I know, and comes to the city to work out just so we get time together. Thank you for being so supportive and offering so much feedback and help. You get me.
- My friends who started as a neighborhood crew, and now feel like a core part of my life. You make my life easier and better. Thank you for the random meet-ups and for the joy you bring to my life.

- My three brothers-in-law and two sisters-in-law. I've always felt lucky to have you in my life. Your love, friendship, and support mean the world to me.
- My uncles, aunts, cousins, and step-siblings from birth and marriage. I feel grateful to be surrounded by so much love and so many memories.
- My grandparents, who have passed. Your love, your stories, and your quiet strength continue to live on in me. I carry you in my heart and in these pages.
- Izzy's care team and my own care team. Thank you for walking beside me, helping me heal, holding space, and believing in my voice. You were part of this process in ways you may never fully know.

To my mom: I chose you. You have always been the best listener and my most unwavering supporter. You push me to see things in myself that I sometimes can't. Your love is unconditional, and I feel it in everything you do. Thank you for being the best Yaya to Izzy. You found a great partner in Mitchell, and I'm so lucky to have a wonderful stepdad. Izzy is lucky to have an amazing Grandpa, too.

To my dad: You live life in the present, and I've always admired that. You never let too much time pass without calling and checking in on me. You always made life fun, and that joy stays with me. To my stepmom, Cindy: Thank you for your presence in my life over the years.

To my sister: Thank you for being on this journey with me. You *get it* more than anyone else. I don't know how I would have done life without you. You offer honest feedback, unwavering support, and love that is real and constant. You're an incredible mom, and I'm so proud to walk beside you.

To Izzy: You are light. Wise beyond your years. I love

watching you grow into the beautiful human you are, inside and out. You are my greatest teacher, especially in your ability to laugh, to be present, and to find joy in the moment.

And finally, to the person I chose to spend my life with, my husband: Thank you. You believed in this book from the very beginning. You encouraged me to keep going, even when agents said it wouldn't sell. You have supported every dream, no matter how uncertain the path. You make life fun. You find the joy. You work on yourself and us to be the best husband and dad possible. You keep on trying even when things are hard. And you will always be the number one draft pick at any party. Your mom is smiling down on us—I know she is proud.

From Ali Mann Stevens

I've always dreamed of writing a book that would help others feel heard, understood, and less alone. After the unimaginable loss of my first two children and the journey that followed, this book became a way to honor that pain and the healing that came after. I could not have completed this deeply personal project without the unwavering support of my village, and there are many people I'd like to thank.

To Camille, my partner in crime and co-author: This book would not exist without you. From the moment we met at LinkedIn, I felt an immediate connection to your warmth, compassion, and authenticity. What began as a professional relationship quickly evolved into a cherished friendship—one that deepened through shared loss and meaningful conversations about purpose and healing.

When we reconnected after I lost my twins, I could never have imagined that our shared experiences and passion would give rise to something as profound as *Maternal Hope*. Thank you for being the backbone of this project—for your unwavering commitment, your remarkable leadership, and your ability to bring our vision to life with grace and clarity.

I trust you like a sister and am deeply honored that you trust me in return. Walking this journey with you has been both humbling and a true gift. I will always be grateful that you said "let's do it" when I asked you to write this book with me.

To my husband, Tim: There is no one in this world for whom I am more grateful. From the way we navigated grief in the beginning to the way we continue to hold it with tenderness today, what we share is sacred—and ours alone.

Thank you for encouraging me to follow through on this book, for standing firmly behind my work, and for cheering on every passion I pursue. Because of you, I know what love truly means. Because of you, I am the mother I always hoped I'd be. Because of you, I believe more deeply in myself and what I can accomplish. I worry less, say yes more, and wake each day with gratitude simply because it begins beside you.

Saying yes to marrying you was the best decision of my life. I truly won the lottery the day you asked me to spend it with you.

To Teddy and Ava: Thank you for choosing me to be your mom. You are the miracles that followed my deepest heartbreak—the living proof that hope can bloom even after the darkest storms.

One day, you will learn that there were two children who came before you, and I hope our story of resilience and love inspires you. Your hugs, your laughter, your kisses, and your bright smiles are my greatest comfort and my truest joy.

You remind me every single day why this book, *Maternal Hope*, matters—because you are my hope made real.

To my parents, Janet and Howie Mann: Your love is a force that could move mountains. Thank you for holding space for my tears, for listening without judgment, and for reminding me to breathe when it felt like the air was slipping away. Your unwavering support—not only for this book, but for every chapter of my life—has meant more to me than words can capture.

Your joy, your pride, and your deep interest in everything that matters to me have been a guiding light. I have many hopes for my children, but above all, I want them to feel my love as completely and unconditionally as I have felt yours.

I feel profoundly blessed to be your daughter. Thank you for being my biggest champions. Even as a grown woman, I treasure the chance to make you proud, and I hope I continue to bring joy to your lives each day. I love you both, deeply and endlessly.

To Mendy and Terry, my parents-in-law: Thank you for the unwavering love and faith you have shown our family. Your example of compassion and devotion helped shape Tim into the man he is today—someone who loves deeply and stands strong in life's hardest moments. I see your influence in him every single day.

Thank you for raising him with such tenderness, and for dropping everything to board the first flight from Washington to New York the moment you heard about Liv's condition. Your daily prayers, your steady presence, and your instinct to show up without hesitation brought us comfort beyond words.

I wish you had the chance to meet Max before he passed, but I will always hold close the memory of you holding Liv's hand and kissing her before she took her last breath. It's no mystery where Tim gets his kindness and purity—he is a reflection of the love he was raised in.

To my brother-in-law Jason and sister-in-law Tiff, and your beautiful families: Even though distance kept us physically apart during some of our hardest moments, I always felt your love surrounding us. I have no doubt that if you had lived closer, you would have been by our side every step of the way. I feel incredibly fortunate to have extended family who hold us so deeply in their hearts.

Thank you for helping us honor Liv and Max by

spreading their ashes. That sacred act—and your presence in that moment—is something I will carry with me always. Your love means more to me than words can express.

To my brother David and sister-in-law Sam: Thank you for being the most positive, grounded, and understanding older brother and sister-in-law I could ever ask for.

David, you're the one who always shows up—no questions asked—and I deeply admire the way you lead with quiet courage and unwavering loyalty.

Sam, you are the older sister I never had. Your strength and grace, especially through your own courageous cancer journey, inspire me every day. You just *get* me, often without my needing to say a word. Our family grew richer the moment you became part of it, and I'm so grateful to have you in my life.

Thank you both for setting such a beautiful example as parents, and for loving my children as if they were your own. I know sibling relationships aren't always easy, and I never take ours for granted. I love you both so much.

To my sister Stephie and brother-in-law Freddie: Thank you for being such a special part of my life. Stephie, thank you for opening your heart to both my joy and my sorrow, for celebrating every win with me, and for being the steady, reliable best friend I can always rely on. When my babies were sick, I knew it broke your heart, and that unspoken sisterly connection means more than words can express. Sisterhood is a beautiful thing, and so are you. I love raising our kids together and sharing all of the new experiences parenthood is offering us.

Freddie, thank you for accepting me exactly as I am, quirks and all, and for always bringing the laughter and party. You've earned the title of "Ali Mann's #1 fan," and I'm so glad our family has you. I know you understand grief in a personal way, and I know your dad is proud of the man you've become. I love you both so much.

To my closest friends: They say friends are the family we choose, and I couldn't have asked for a more loving, loyal, and compassionate circle to hold me up. I will never forget the shiva call you organized for Liv and Max—sitting six feet apart in a park, masked, in the height of the pandemic—finding a way to be close when everything felt so far away. You brought meals, sent flowers and essentials, and made sure I never felt alone. Your love surrounded me when I needed it most, and I will carry that with me forever. Thank you for continuing to say Liv and Max's names, for remembering their birthdays and anniversaries, and for showing up again and again with tenderness and strength. I am endlessly grateful.

To my LinkedIn colleagues and friends, as well as the company itself, which shaped me during one of the most defining seasons of my life: I began my journey as a parent while working there, and I'm thankful for the knowledge, support, and space that LinkedIn provided to help me grow both personally and professionally. LinkedIn showed me that it's possible to love your work and honor your family, and that the two don't have to exist in conflict.

A special thank you to Tessa del Rio and Suzanne Krakover, my manager and peer when I prematurely delivered Liv and Max. You stepped in with such grace and conviction, taking over my team so I could grieve and begin to heal. Your leadership and humanity made all the difference. To my LTS, LLS, and LSS colleagues who honored my babies by sending engraved jewelry, naming stars, sending flowers, and most importantly, showing deep respect for "family first"—thank you. Your gestures were filled with compassion, one of LinkedIn's greatest leadership values.

And finally, if it weren't for LinkedIn, I would never have met Camille—my co-author, creative partner, and dear friend —and *Maternal Hope* wouldn't exist. For that, and so much more, I am endlessly thankful.

To Liv and Max: Thank you for the profound honor of being your mom. Because of your brief-yet-meaningful time on this earth, and all that we experienced together, I am stronger, braver, and more resilient than I ever would have been without you. You've given me a new perspective on life— one filled with gratitude, grace, and a deep appreciation for even the smallest moments.

I hold the memory of your beautiful porcelain faces close, often afraid they might fade—but even after five years, those images remain crystal clear in my mind. Thank you for the signs, for visiting me in dreams, and for somehow making it possible to conceive Teddy and Ava naturally. I know in my soul that you had a hand in their arrival. It was no coincidence. You will always be my firstborns. I love you endlessly.

RESOURCES FOR READERS

In this section, we've compiled a list of resources, categorized to help you find the support you need including some of the ones that helped our authors.

Children with Disabilities

Websites

- Childcare.gov (childcare.gov)
- Center for Parent Information and Resources (parentcenterhub.org)

Books

- *Expecting Adam: A True Story of Birth, Rebirth, and Everyday Magic*, by Martha Beck
- *Far from the Tree: Parents, Children, and the Search for Identity*, by Andrew Solomon
- *Uniquely Human: A Different Way of Seeing Autism*, by Barry M. Prizant

Podcasts

- *The Lucky Few*

Fertility and Infertility

<u>Websites</u>

- American Society for Reproductive Medicine (asrm.org)
- CCRM (CCRMivf.com)
- FertilityIQ (fertilityiq.com)
- Gateway Women (gateway-women.com)
- Maven Health (mavenclinic.com)
- Not So Mommy... (notsomommy.com)
- Resolve: The National Infertility Association (resolve.org)

<u>Books</u>

- *It Starts with the Egg: The Science of Egg Quality for Fertility, Miscarriage, and IVF,* by Rebecca Fett
- *Living the Life Unexpected: 12 Weeks to Your Plan B for a Meaningful and Fulfilling Future Without Children,* by Jody Day
- *Own Your Fertility: From Egg Freezing to Surrogacy, How to Take Charge of Your Body and Your Future,* by Jaime Knopman and Rebecca Raphael
- *Taking Charge of Your Fertility: The Definitive Guide to Natural Birth Control, Pregnancy Achievement, and Reproductive Health,* by Toni Weschler

<u>Podcasts</u>

- *As a Woman*
- *Big Fat Negative*
- *Fertility Friday Podcast*
- *Infertile AF*

- *Infertility Feelings*

Miscarriage, Stillbirth, and Child Loss

<u>Websites</u>

- Compassionate Friends (compassionatefriends.org)
- The Miscarriage Association (miscarriageassociation.org.uk)
- Star Legacy Foundation (starlegacyfoundation.org)

<u>Books</u>

- *An Exact Replica of a Figment of My Imagination*, by Elizabeth McCracken
- *Empty Arms: Hope and Support for Those Who Have Suffered a Miscarriage, Stillbirth, or Tubal Pregnancy*, by Pam Vredevelt
- *I Had a Miscarriage: A Memoir, a Movement*, by Jessica Zucker, PhD
- *Pregnancy after Loss*, by Zoe Clark Coates
- *Shattered: Surviving the Loss of a Child*, by Gary Roe

Postpartum Depression

<u>Websites</u>

- Postpartum Support International (postpartum.net)

<u>Books</u>

- *Down Came the Rain: My Journey Through Postpartum Depression*, by Brooke Shields

- *The Fourth Trimester: A Postpartum Guide to Healing Your Body, Balancing Your Emotions, and Restoring Your Vitality*, by Kimberly Ann Johnson
- *The Postpartum Depression Workbook: Strategies to Overcome Negative Thoughts, Feelings, and Behaviors*, by Pamela S. Wiegartz and Kevin L. Gyoerkoe
- *This Isn't What I Expected: Overcoming Postpartum Depression*, by Karen R. Kleiman and Valerie Davis Raskin

Surrogacy

Websites

- American Surrogacy (americansurrogacy.com)
- Surrogate.com (surrogate.com)

Books

- *Experiencing Surrogacy: Perspective and Advice from a Surrogate's and Intended Parent's Pregnancy Journey Together*, by Emily Dublin Field and Melissa Fleck
- *Surrogacy Was the Way: Twenty Intended Mothers Tell Their Stories*, by Zara Griswold

Other

Websites

- Chick Mission (thechickmission.org)
- Endo Mission (endomission.org)
- Family Equality (familyequality.org)
- Gays With Kids (gayswithkids.com)
- Lily Concierge (lilyconcierge.com)

- Men Having Babies (menhavingbabies.org)
- Tommy's (tommys.org)

Books

- *Normalize It: Upending the Silence, Stigma, and Shame That Shape Women's Lives*, by Jessica Zucker, PhD
- *The Fifth Trimester*, by Lauren Smith Brody
- *Our NICU Journey: A Four Week NICU Journal*, by Trish Ringley
- *The Unexpected: Navigating Pregnancy During and After Complications*, by Emily Oyster
- *What No One Tells You*, by Alexandra Sacks and Catherine Birndorf

Podcasts

- *After Bedtime with Big Little Feelings*
- *Empowering NICU Parents Podcast*
- *Good Inside with Dr. Becky*
- *The Motherly Podcast*

ABOUT CAMILLE SEIGLE

Camille Seigle is a consultant, mentor, speaker, and facilitator who helps guide individuals and companies to unlock their full potential. She uses intuitive approaches and holds clients accountable to their goals to foster personalized growth and success. Drawing on a rich professional background that began in hospitality and continued at LinkedIn, Camille brings warmth, clarity, and structure to her coaching work. She holds a B.A. from Denison University, a postgraduate diploma from Les Roches Global Hospitality Education, and an Organizational and Leadership Coaching Certificate from Northwestern University. Certified by the International Coaching Federation, Camille integrates values, longevity, and holistic assessment tools into her practice to support clients in building more balanced and fulfilling lives.

Camille's postpartum experience left her feeling alone and isolated during the COVID-19 pandemic. Returning to work remotely after maternity leave didn't help. She believes that many of us are holding our most painful stories close, despite the fact that so many people are going through similar challenges. She believes in the power of sharing our stories and hopes this anthology allows many to recognize that they are not alone in their experiences.

Camille lives in Chicago with her husband and their daughter. She loves to travel, spend time with her family, and nurture her mind, body, and soul. This is her first book.

Connect with Camille at MyMaternalHope.com.

ABOUT ALI MANN STEVENS

Ali Mann Stevens is a sales leader at a fast-growing tech company. She is a *summa cum laude* graduate of Queens College, where she earned a degree in sociology before unexpectedly finding her way into the world of sales. What began as a college job selling Cutco evolved into a fulfilling career—including over a decade at LinkedIn—where she discovered a passion for building high-performing teams and empowering others to reach their full potential.

Her journey took a profoundly personal turn after the premature birth and tragic loss of her twins, who were born at twenty-six and a half weeks—an experience that left her feeling isolated until she discovered comfort in the stories of others who had walked similar paths. The realization that none of us are ever truly alone became her inspiration for this book, in which she offers strength, connection, and hope to others navigating the often silent struggles of parenthood.

Ali lives with deep gratitude for the life she holds: a loving partner, two healthy children, a supportive family, and the lessons that loss and love have taught her. When she's not writing or working, she enjoys family adventures outdoors, traveling, painting, interior design, and pausing to appreciate the simple beauty of everyday moments.

Originally from Long Island, New York, Ali now lives in Westchester County with her husband, Tim, and their two young children, Teddy and Ava. This is her first book.

Connect with Ali at MyMaternalHope.com.

www.ingramcontent.com/pod-product-compliance
Lightning Source LLC
Chambersburg PA
CBHW031502120626
46545CB00005B/1713